CW01367653

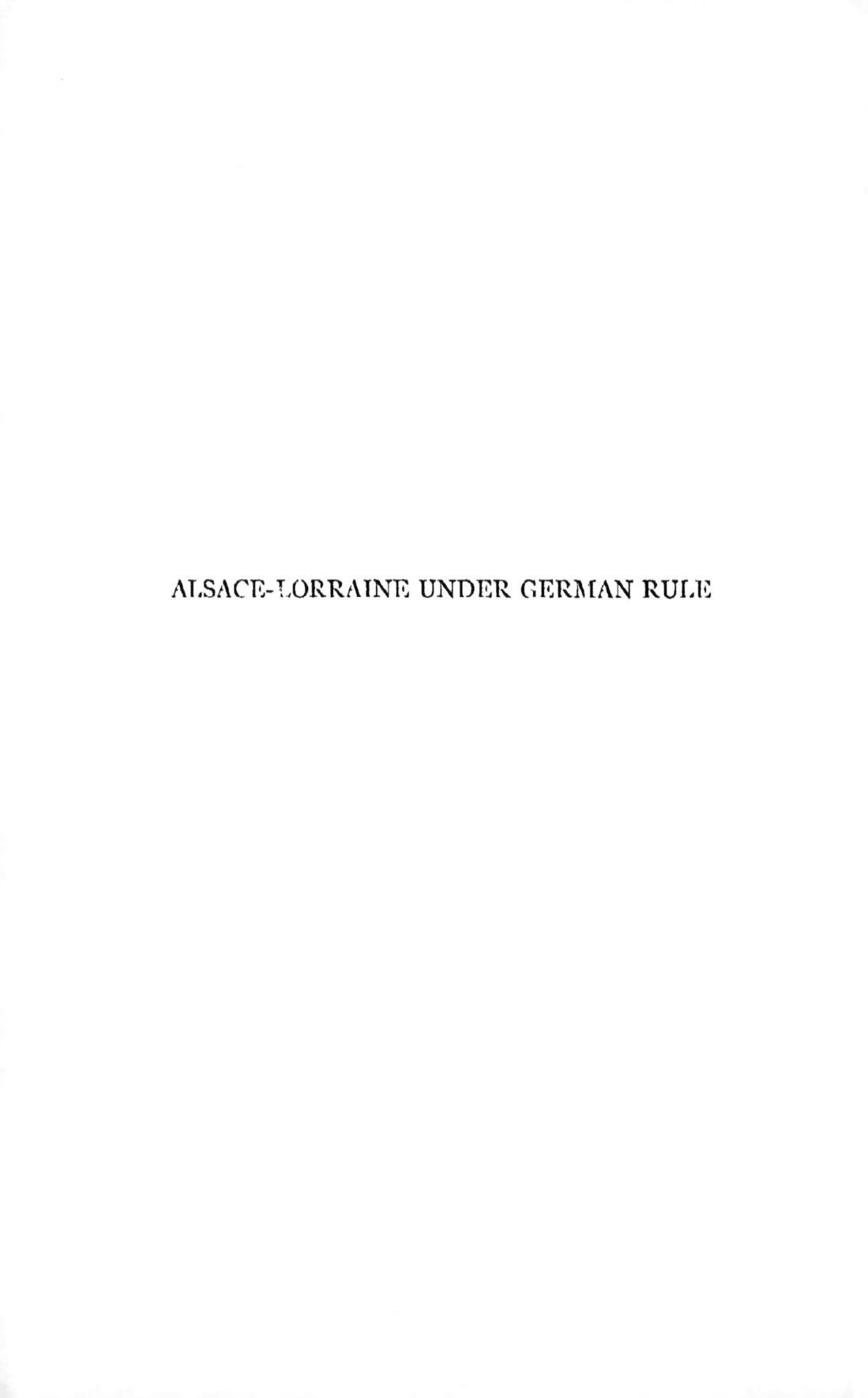

ALSACE-LORRAINE UNDER GERMAN RULE

ALSACE-LORRAINE
UNDER GERMAN RULE

BY
CHARLES DOWNER HAZEN
PROFESSOR OF HISTORY IN COLUMBIA UNIVERSITY

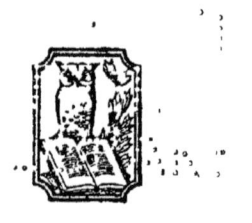

NEW YORK
HENRY HOLT AND COMPANY
1917

COPYRIGHT, 1917
BY
HENRY HOLT AND COMPANY

Published November, 1917

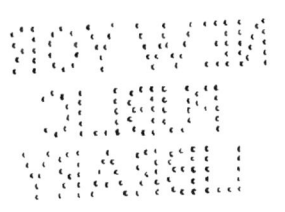

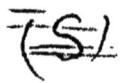

CONTENTS

CHAPTER	PAGE
I. The Treaty of Frankfort	3
II. Alsace-Lorraine before the Treaty of Frankfort	20
III. Why Germany Annexed Alsace-Lorraine	78
IV. The Victim's Privilege	97
V. Alsace-Lorraine, 1871–1890	108
VI. Alsace-Lorraine, 1890–1911	139
VII. The Constitution of 1911	175
VIII. The Saverne Affair	189
IX. Conclusion	215
Index	237

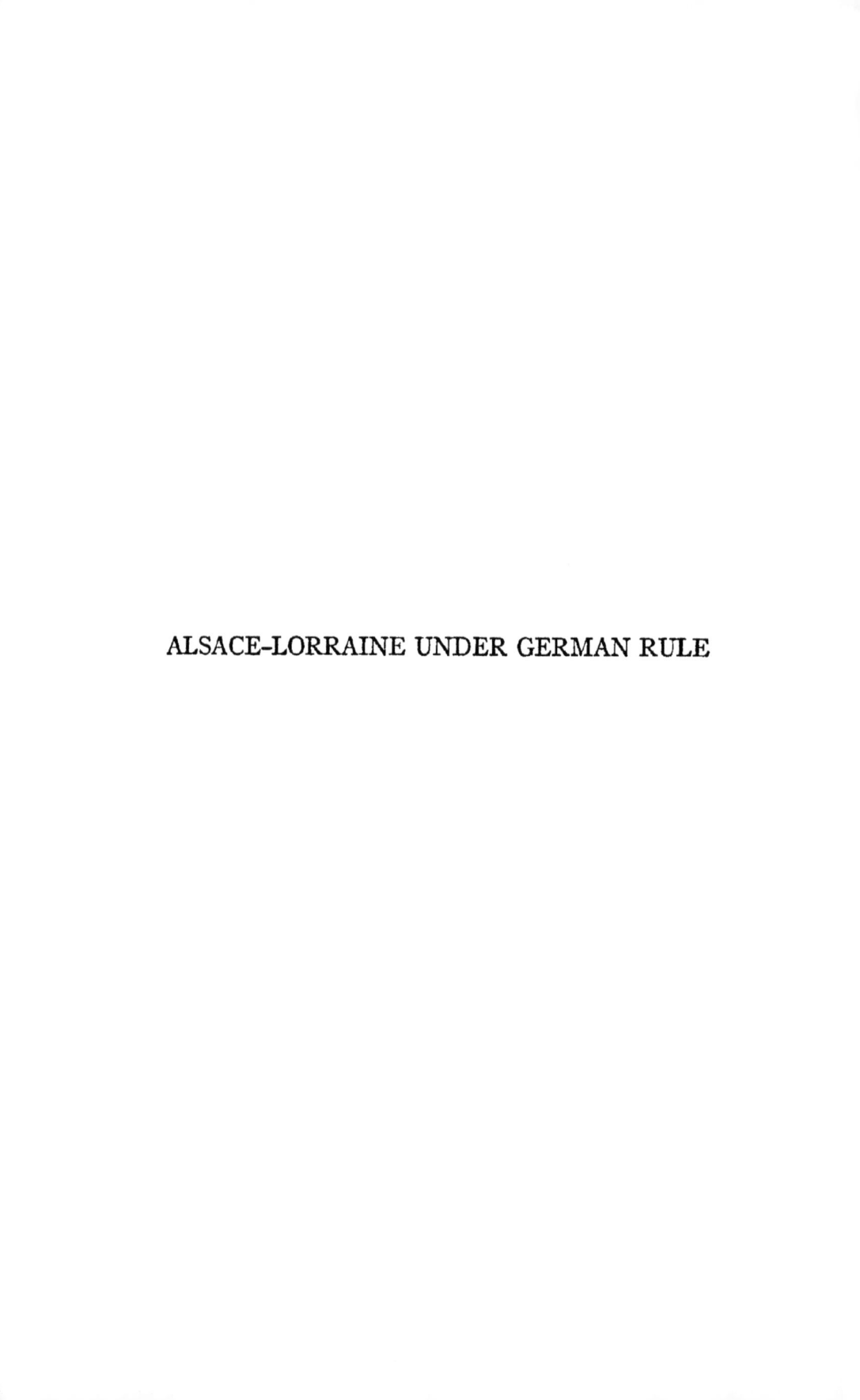

ALSACE-LORRAINE UNDER GERMAN RULE

"Modern Europe cannot allow a people to be seized like a herd of cattle. . . ."
> *Protest of Alsace-Lorraine against Annexation to Germany, delivered in the National Assembly at Bordeaux, February 17, 1871.*

"Citizens, possessed of souls and of intelligence, are not merchandise to be traded and therefore it is not lawful to make them the subject of a contract."
> *Protest of Alsace-Lorraine against Annexation to Germany, delivered in the Reichstag in Berlin, February 18, 1874.*

"No right exists anywhere to hand peoples about from sovereignty to sovereignty as if they were property."
> *Address of President Wilson to the Senate of the United States, January 22, 1917.*

CHAPTER I

THE TREATY OF FRANKFORT

"FRANCE renounces, in favor of the German Empire, all rights and titles to the territories situated east of the frontier designated below.

"The German Empire shall possess these territories forever, in full sovereignty and ownership."

Such was Article 1 of the Treaty of Frankfort of May 10, 1871, which closed the Franco-German war, a treaty which the French Government was compelled to sign and the French National Assembly to ratify under compulsion as peremptory and as complete as any nation has experienced in modern times. That treaty terminated a war which Bismarck, in his autobiography, claims the honor and the glory of having caused, a treaty which he handed as a brilliant and substantial trophy to the new German Empire, proclaimed in the great Hall of Mirrors in the Palace of Versailles on January 18, 1871, an empire therefore less than four months old. This memorable birthday gift was destined to exert a decisive and enduring influence upon the character of the young recipient and to prove a heavy heritage for modern Europe. It was to set an indelible mark upon all subsequent history, covering the face of the earth with its menace, exacting a continuous and increasing tribute of costly sacrifice from millions and millions of human beings who have paid it in fear and trembling.

There were at the time Frenchmen of high standing in the realm of thought and action who urged the Assembly never to sign this fateful document; Gambetta, soul of the national defense, flaming, dynamic embodiment of the resolution of a people at bay, who had accomplished prodigies during the war, but not quite prodigies enough, and who demanded war to the bitter end, believing that that end would be less bitter than the alternative now offered; Louis Blanc who appealed, in vain, for a people's war, for a repetition of the epic of 1793 when the nation rose *en masse* and threw back the invader, a kind of war which the German General Staff feared above everything, as it later admitted; Edgar Quinet who called the attention of the Assembly to the new frontier as both illogical and dangerous, a veritable dagger pointed at the heart of France; and who correctly prophesied the future, war always latent, immanent in the nature of things, ruinous armaments heavier in the long run than any present efforts would be; and who pointed out the shameful dishonor in this buying of peace by the cession of three departments, the abandonment of a part of the nation that the rest might be free.

But these were not the voices heard above the tumult of the times. The Assembly of Bordeaux took counsel of an imperative situation. The unparalleled and comprehensive disasters of the war left it no alternative, if it would avoid the complete annihilation of the independence of the country. Swift submission to the demands of an enemy everywhere triumphant seemed to the great majority the only method of keeping open the door of the future for the stricken country. Otherwise short shrift would be made of the victim now in the hands of a state it was powerless to repel, and the future condition of the nation would be worse than the present. Mutilation was preferable to extinction. Believing the dilemma inexorable, and holding that discretion was the truer wisdom, as well as the greater heroism, the Assembly, with a heavy heart, ratified the treaty by a vote of 433 to 98.

Thus were ceded to Germany all of Alsace, save Belfort, and a considerable part of Lorraine, in all 1,694 villages, towns and cities, 1,597,538 human beings, 5,600 square miles of territory, a region nearly as large as Connecticut and Rhode Island. The boundary had been traced months before which was now substantially followed. As early as September, 1870, before the bombardment of Strasburg, before the capitulation of Metz, a map had been published in Berlin which had been prepared by the geographical and statistical division of the General Staff. It was the famous map "with the green border." With slight modification, the green border stood on the maps appended to the Treaty of Frankfort practically as in this initial sketch. During the negotiations of the final terms of peace, the French had pressed intensely for a better boundary; but their efforts had been in vain. Concessions are made to the strong, not to the weak.

Such was the famous transaction—the annexation of Alsace and Lorraine to Germany. The result of a war, incorporated in a treaty bearing a definite date and containing an explicit definition of the thing transferred, it was a *fait accompli*. Thus was projected into European politics a most vexatious problem, the question of Alsace-Lorraine, a question the very existence of which, however, official and popular Germany has steadily denied. Planting herself firmly upon Article 1 of the Treaty of

Frankfort, Germany has stood immovable, and as if impregnable. For her there was henceforth "nothing to discuss" concerning these territories, now cut off from France. For her "the question of Alsace-Lorraine does not exist." In 1892, the Parisian newspaper, *Le Figaro*, had the futile idea of questioning a number of important Germans about this matter. Here is the reply of the President of the Reichstag, Herr von Levetzow. "In your letter of the 24th of last January, you were so kind as to honor me with a series of inquiries concerning the possibility of a peaceful solution of the 'question of Alsace-Lorraine.'

"All these inquiries are answered by the provision of the first article of the peace preliminaries, confirmed by the treaty of May 10, 1871, between France and the German Empire and according to which the regions designated as the territory of Alsace-Lorraine are ceded forever, in complete sovereignty and possession, to the German Empire.

"In referring to this clause of the treaty, I have the honor to beg you to accept the expression of my high esteem."

On August 16, 1888, in inaugurating a monument in honor of Prince Frederick Charles of Prussia at Frankfort-on-the-Oder, the Emperor, William II, who had just ascended the throne, spoke as follows:

"There are those who have shamelessly asserted that my father wished to give back what he and Prince Frederick Charles had together conquered with the sword. We have all known him too well to keep silent for a moment in the face of this insult to his name. He thought, as we think, that none of the conquests of that great period can be abandoned. I believe that we all know that there is only one opinion on that subject, and that we would leave our eighteen army corps dead upon the field of battle rather than yield a single stone of what was won by my father and Prince Frederick Charles."

Between that day and this, there has been with Emperor and with people no variableness, neither shadow of turning, upon this subject. Their attitude has been one of resolute determination, of rigid, uncompromising finality.

Yet it does not take two to raise a question, one will suffice. Despite the studied silence of the victors, tempered now and then with a curt and crushing reference to the Treaty of Frankfort, there *is* a question of Alsace-Lorraine, and there has been one since May 10, 1871. This question has dominated the policy of every nation of Europe, including very particularly the one for which it "does not exist." Its shadow has covered the world. Repeatedly this unwelcome ghost has appeared while the feast has been proceeding, and has frozen the hearts of the revellers with its terrible, mute protest, its demand for expiation.

If, from the German point of view, this question does not exist, why has it been so ardently discussed by those who constantly deny; why, in the lengthy and lengthening bibliography of the subject are there so many German titles? The question was not settled in 1871, it was merely raised. And there are reasons to believe that it will not be settled until it is settled right. The present age ought not to have to be told the elementary truth that nothing is stable which is unjust. If in doubt, it might reflect upon the present status of the question of Poland, supposed to have been "settled" in 1772, 1793 and 1795.

If a treaty gives inalienable and infrangible rights how does it happen that those which France could cite in support of her claims to Alsace and Lorraine, treaties running over two centuries and a half, could be so lightly disregarded? Why should a single treaty alone be definitive? If we refer only to the principal ones we have the following list:

Peace of Cateau-Cambrésis, 1559.
Peace of Westphalia, 1648.
Peace of the Pyrenees, 1659.
Peace of Aix-la-Chapelle, 1668.
Peace of Nimwegen, 1678.
Peace of Ryswick, 1697.
Peace of Utrecht, 1713.
Treaty of Vienna, 1738.
Treaties of Basel, 1795.
Peace of Lunéville, 1801.
Treaties of 1814 and 1815.

Do treaties differ from one another in validity? Is one at liberty to be eclectic in this field and to pick and choose according to one's taste? Even so, one should be reasonably prudent and circumspect and studiously refrain from tearing up one's own title deeds. A war between two nations abrogates all treaties between those two. By declaring war on France in August, 1914, Germany annihilated the Treaty of Frankfort and shattered that boasted support. At least since then there has been, by action of the beneficiary herself, a question of Alsace-Lorraine.

But there has been such a question since 1871. The Armed Peace of 1871-1914 and the World War since 1914, are indubitable proofs of its existence, its virility and its implacability. It has been kept open all these years because it is more than a local question; because it epitomizes in clear and definite fashion the most absorbing preoccupation of the modern world, the aspiration for liberty, for the recognition and establishment of popular rights. The cause of Alsace-Lorraine is the cause of humanity.

The Treaty of Frankfort is a turning point in modern history. Its specific provisions, its underlying doctrine, its import and significance, have had incalculable and most unhappy consequences. That treaty was a sharp and peremptory denial of the modern democratic principle that governments derive their just powers from the consent of the governed, that a people is entitled to be the captain of its own destinies. It was a blunt assertion of the absolute right of physical force in the world, of the good old principle that those shall take who have the power and those shall keep who can.

Against this act, and its primitive philosophy, the people most directly concerned issued a flaming and impotent protest. It was by action of the victims themselves that the question of Alsace-Lorraine was first raised, and with such poignant emphasis that it has ever since haunted the conscience of the world.

The Germans asserted that the incident was closed as soon as the Treaty of Frankfort was signed and ratified. The people of Alsace-Lorraine, on the other hand, asserted that that very act created a question, that it ended nothing, that it enthroned wrong in triumph in the world and was therefore a negation of the moral law, that no wrong can create a right. By the sharpness of the challenge, by the passionate, though unavailing, denunciation of the deed, the people of Alsace-Lorraine defined the issue as one of supreme international morality. They thus rendered a service to humanity in the age-long struggle for justice similar to that rendered in 1914 by the Belgians in their magnificent loyalty to the cause of right.

Even before the official beginnings of the negotiations for the peace between France and Germany, and on February 17, 1871, the deputies in the National Assembly from the menaced departments declared solemnly in the Assembly "the immutable will of Alsace and Lorraine to remain French territory," asserted that France could not agree to or sign the cession of Alsace and Lorraine, that the French people did not have the right to accept such a mutilation, that France might "experience the blows of force, but could not sanction its decrees," that Europe could "neither permit nor ratify the abandonment of Alsace and Lorraine," that it could not allow "the seizure of a people as a common herd" nor permit a peace which would be "a legitimate and permanent provocation to war." The conclusion of this protest was as follows: "Wherefore we call our fellow-citizens of France and the governments and peoples of the entire world to witness in advance that we hold to be null and void every act and treaty, vote or plebiscite, which would consent to the abandonment, in favor of the foreigner, of all or of any part of our provinces of Alsace and Lorraine."

Two weeks later, on March 1, 1871, immediately after the ratification of the preliminaries of peace by the National Assembly, the representatives of the sacrificed provinces again solemnly protested against outraged right. This famous protest, whose passion and whose pathos have since moved all right-thinking men for two generations and ought to arrest and fix the attention of the world to-day, should be read in full.

"The representatives of Alsace and Lorraine submitted to the Assembly, before peace negotiations were begun, a declaration affirming in the most formal way, in the name of the two provinces, their will and their right to remain French.

"Handed over, in contempt of all justice and by an odious abuse of force, to the domination of foreigners, we now have a final duty to perform.

"We declare once more null and void a compact which disposes of us without our consent.

"Henceforth and forever each and every one of us will be completely justified in demanding our rights in whatever way and manner our consciences may approve.

"At the moment of leaving the chamber where our dignity no longer permits us to sit, and in spite of the bitterness of our grief, the supreme thought which we find at the bottom of our hearts is a thought of gratitude to those who, for six months, have not ceased to fight in our defense, and our unalterable attachment to France from which we are torn by violence.

"We shall follow you with our wishes and we shall await with entire confidence in the future, the resumption by a regenerated France of the course of her great destiny.

"Your brothers of Alsace and Lorraine, now cut off from the common family, will preserve for France, absent from their hearths, a filial affection until the day when she shall resume her rightful place there once more."

Three years later, on February 18, 1874, Alsace-Lorraine registered another protest, this time in the very capital of the victor, in Berlin. For three years Germany had ruled with an iron hand this country which she pretended to have "liberated," this home of her long-lost "brothers." Scores of thousands of Alsatians and Lorrainers had left their native land and scores of thousands of Germans had entered it. Yet in the very first elections to the Reichstag after the war, Alsace and Lorraine, entitled to fifteen members in the Reichstag, elected fifteen men whose first act after they reached Berlin was to protest formally before the Reichstag against the change of nationality forced upon them by the conqueror.

This protest was preceded by a proposition, to wit: "May it please the Reichstag to decide:

"That the people of Alsace-Lorraine, incorporated without their consent in the German Empire by the Treaty of Frankfort, be called upon to pronounce themselves upon this incorporation."

The protest itself was in the following words: "The people of Alsace-Lorraine, whom we represent in the Reichstag, have entrusted us with a special and very weighty mission, which we wish to discharge at once. They have charged us with expressing to you their thought in regard to the change of nationality which has been violently imposed upon them as a result of your war with France.

"Your last war, which ended to the advantage of your nation, gave it incontestably the right to reparation. But Germany has exceeded her right as a civilized nation in forcing conquered France to sacrifice a million and a half of her children.

"If, in times remote and comparatively barbarous, the right of conquest has sometimes been transformed into effective right; if, even to-day, it is pardoned when exercised on ignorant and savage peoples, nothing of this sort can be applied to Alsace-Lorraine. It is at the end of the nineteenth century, of a century of light and progress, that Germany conquers us, and the people whom she has reduced to slavery—for annexation without our consent is for us a veritable moral slavery—this people is one of the best of Europe, perhaps the people which is most devoted to the sentiment of right and justice.

"Do you argue that the treaty ceding to you our territory and its inhabitants was concluded regularly and in due form? But reason, no less than the most ordinary principles of right, declares that such a treaty cannot be valid. Citizens, possessed of souls and of intelligence, are not merchandise to be traded and therefore it is not lawful to make them the subject of a contract. Moreover, even admitting—what we do not admit—that France had the right to cede us, the compact which you cite against us possesses no validity. A contract is only valid when it represents the free will of the contracting parties. Now it was only when the knife was at her throat, that France, bleeding and exhausted, signed the treaty abandoning us. She was not free, she yielded only to force, and our codes of law inform us that violence nullifies any agreements tainted by it.

"To give an appearance of legality to the cession of Alsace-Lorraine, the least that you ought to have done would have been to submit that cession to the ratification of the people ceded.

"A celebrated jurist, Professor Bluntschli of Heidelberg, in his International Law (p. 285) says; 'In order that a cession of land be valid, the recognition by the people inhabiting the land ceded and in the possession of political rights is necessary. This recognition can never be omitted or suppressed, because peoples are not things without rights or wills of their own, whose property may be disposed of by others.'

"You see, Gentlemen, that we find nothing in the teachings of morality and justice, absolutely nothing, which can pardon our annexation to your empire; and in this our reasons are in harmony with our sentiments. Our hearts, are in fact, irresistibly attracted toward our French fatherland. Two centuries of life and of thought together create, between the members of the same family, a sacred bond which no argument and much less any act of violence can destroy.

"By choosing us, feeling as we all do, our electors have above everything else desired to affirm their sympathy for their French fatherland and their right to dispose of themselves."

Such was the unanimous protest of the fifteen delegates of Alsace-Lorraine to the first Reichstag in which they sat. It was not even listened to with the respect due the vanquished. Laughter, guffaws, and interruptions, which almost prevented the spokesman from being heard, revealed the amount of magnanimity possessed by the members of the Reichstag. Men who do not honor others do not honor themselves. The next day the *Frankfurter Zeitung* protested against the disgraceful tumult, the ironical laughter that had accompanied the reading of the protest.

In July, 1917, a Socialist deputy of the Reichstag is reported to have said: "In the eyes of all Socialists what occurred in 1871 was nothing else than the return of these fundamentally German provinces into the bosom of the great German family. During the entire course of the war, that party to which I belong has considered as a self-evident principle that the total or the partial cession of Alsace-Lorraine was not at all open to discussion. For every German Socialist, the question of Alsace-Lorraine was definitely settled in 1871."

But in 1871 the leaders of the Socialist party, Bebel and Liebknecht, to their everlasting credit, protested against the annexation of Alsace-Lorraine. They were forthwith put in prison for having maintained their opinion in speeches and in writings.

By Germany's insistence upon the cession of Alsace-Lorraine in 1871, and by these repeated protests of the people of Alsace-Lorraine against that act, a new and highly disturbing element was introduced into the history of Europe, nor has it yet been eliminated.

CHAPTER II

ALSACE-LORRAINE BEFORE THE TREATY OF FRANKFORT

WHAT was this country, now transferred as a war prize, in its essential character, in its fundamental nature? Was it German or was it French? The question has received two answers. The Germans have asserted that it was German, the French that it was French. The opinion of those most intimately concerned, the people of Alsace and Lorraine themselves, was just as explicit as either of these. They asserted, as we have seen, that they were French and wished to remain French, and that the document that pretended to transfer them was from the start and would forever remain null and void.

What light did history throw upon this problem, if it was a problem? It is impossible within the confines of this volume to recount with any fulness the crowded annals of this people. The story does not easily lend itself to compression, it is so long, so varied, and so involved. Nevertheless, out of its bewildering intricacies, a few features in the slow evolution may profitably be noticed. They may serve to indicate with reasonable certitude the individuality of these provinces, which was the product of manifold forces, operating, sometimes obscurely, sometimes clearly, through the course of many centuries. For, that Alsace and Lorraine had personalities of their own is obvious to any frank and serious student, and even a brief analysis of the various strains of experience that entered into the formation of them ought to prove instructive.

Who the first inhabitants were of these regions between the river Meuse, the Vosges mountains, and the Rhine, it is idle to inquire. In the dim background of European history groups of human beings flit obscurely, appearing and then disappearing, leaving only a few tantalizing and dubious traces of their passage. Ethnology gives us only an elusive guidance through those remote mazes of time. But with the coming of the Romans, we find ourselves on fairly solid ground. Thanks to Julius Cæsar, to his victories and his writings, these regions of Europe pass out of the penumbra into the light of authentic history. And Cæsar lived in the first century before Christ.

He found there a population that was Celtic, which had, however, even before he appeared upon the scene, experienced the repeated shock of attempted invasion from beyond the Rhine by another branch of the great Aryan race, the Teutonic. Cæsar's conquests added Gaul to the Roman Empire and fixed its boundary at the river Rhine. For nearly five centuries the Rhine remained the boundary between Gaul and independent and barbarous Germania. The "Roman Peace" was thus imposed upon what we know to-day as Alsace and Lorraine.

It was under such illustrious auspices that these lands made their real début into history. With this Celtic-Roman population some German elements were mingled, in what proportion it would be impossible to say. Roman colonists, governmental, military, and commercial, brought with them the characteristic elements of Roman civilization. Here, as elsewhere, some of the great routes, over which men still travel, were Roman roads. Agriculture, industry, and commerce felt the vivifying touch of Rome. Roman deities came to compete with older and cruder principalities and powers in the favor of myth-making men. Some they chased away, others they absorbed and transformed. Roman cities were founded which are still the busy haunts of men, Metz, Toul, Verdun, Strasburg, Saverne. From the third century vines were planted, whose product was consumed in the country or sold to the neighboring Germans across the Rhine. Pottery, arms, textiles were exchanged for other things with the various tribes that lived along the river courses. Roman officials, Roman soldiers, Roman inn-keepers and money-changers, Roman mariners, plied their various trades in these lands which were then and have always been considered exceptionally endowed by nature. The population naturally lost all independent existence, absorbed in the mighty and universal empire. From the third century onward Christianity gradually penetrated these plains and valleys.

From the third century also dated the renewal of attacks from Germany. Rome, in the long run, did not have the necessary strength to defend the frontiers of Gaul and with the fifth century the boasted ramparts of her power, the Rhine and the Danube, gave way. The Teutonic floods poured in, wave after wave, and the face of Europe was changed.

These Teutonic invasions continued intermittently for several centuries. Southward to the Mediterranean, westward to the Atlantic came tribe after tribe, each seeking a warmer, a more congenial place in the sun. When these torrential incursions of primitive barbarism were over, the face of Europe was profoundly and permanently altered. With the native stocks of western and southern Europe were blended new racial strains. With the creation of a changed population, resulting from the fusion of conquerors and conquered, came also new ideas and customs which transformed, in the domains of politics and society, the older, more orderly, more elaborate and more rational civilization of ancient Rome. The first rough and uncertain outlines of new nations were gradually sketched against a background of moving, restless, obscure masses of human beings which had hitherto played no ascertainable historical rôle but which were now cooperating in strange, blind, stumbling ways in the inauguration of a new phase of history. Out of the chaos and the darkness of this Wandering of the Peoples a new cosmos gradually emerged. From this infiltration of Teutonic racial elements and peculiar Teutonic institutions into an empire of different racial elements and different institutions proceeded in time the turbid, turbulent stream of history which we call that of the Middle Ages, an absorbing and difficult chapter, a few only of whose outstanding features can be considered here.

The country between the Vosges and the Rhine, with whose destinies we are particularly concerned, was inundated by these floods. The ancient Roman civilization, and probably the incipient Christianity, of Alsace were swept away. The ancient population either fled to the comparatively safe valleys of the Vosges, or was reduced to slavery or serfdom by the conquerors. Alsace relapsed into its former state of primitive barbarism.

Long and confused struggles between Allamans and Franks, resulting finally in the victory of the latter, and in the reintroduction of Christianity into this region, resulting, also, in the appearance of new leaders, called dukes and counts, and in the creation of ecclesiastical domains around monasteries and bishoprics, furnished outer evidences of the inner changes in the constitution of society. In time there appeared the imposing figure of Charlemagne trying with temporary success to weld all these disparate and centrifugal elements of western and northern Europe into a single state, trying, also, to push its boundaries farther and farther east by driving back the Slavs and other strange breeds of men. Particularly did Charlemagne influence all subsequent history by attempting to renew the Roman Empire whose mighty memories still haunted the minds of men, holding them in thrall to its elusive, indestructible fascination. On Christmas Day in the year 800 and in the church of St. Peter at Rome, Charlemagne was crowned Emperor of Rome by the Pope, an old title now applied to a very different state.

Charlemagne's empire did not last long after his death. The centrifugal forces were too strong for any attempt at European unification to succeed, even when aided by the powerful patronage of the Pope.

After a confused period of dislocation and readjustment and the practical transfer of the new title to a line of German princes there appeared that shimmering and half phantasmal institution known as the Holy Roman Empire, which lived its peculiar life all through the Middle Ages and down into modern times, until it encountered the wilful personality of Napoleon, who, for reasons of his own, gave it its quietus in 1806.

The Holy Roman Empire was far smaller in its range than the empire of Charlemagne had been. It did not include what came to be known as France, a region which had, in the dominant centrifugalism of the times, escaped and was threading its own way toward kingdom and toward unity. The Holy Roman Empire was really a German Empire with indefinite pretensions to the control of Italy, which pretensions it, in the end, could not make good. But the reader should not for a moment imagine that this German Empire of the Middle Ages was the father of the German Empire of to-day, and that the latter is the lawful legatee of the former. It may satisfy the historic sense of modern Germans to see in the Hohenzollerns inheritors and incarnators of the secular traditions of the Hohenstauffen and the Hapsburgs. Such conceptions can only appear fallacious to the student who is interested in seeing the past as it was, and not in complacently burnishing a grandiose and flattering legend.

The Holy Roman Empire was a confederation and a confederation lacking in both material and moral unity. Within it were included states of every rank and grade, of every size and shape, of every degree of weakness and of strength. Some of the states were included only in part within the confederation, other parts lying outside its boundaries. It was a marvellous mosaic, but without the cement that holds the pieces of a mosaic in place, a conglomeration of petty units, appearing, disappearing, absorbed or splitting off, in endless permutations and combinations during the thousand years of its generally diaphanous existence. Nothing about it was static, little about it was impressive. Its lofty and sweeping pretensions were in ironic contrast with its actual power. The map of Germany was a bewildering collection of patches of color. This empire was the product of feudalism and it illustrated better than any other state in Europe the destructive capacity which lay in the feudal principle, the extreme diffusion, dispersion, dilution of power, the ineradicable tendency to break up into endless particles, combining and dissolving, according to the laws of attraction and repulsion, into innumerable centers of fragile and ephemeral life. A glance at the map of this empire at any moment between 800 and 1800 A. D. will show why the Empire represented only a maximum of pretensions, a minimum of power.

It is said that there were at one time over three hundred and fifty states within the Empire, kingdoms, counties, duchies, margraviates, bishoprics, principalities, and free imperial cities. From the political point of view it was an organism of a low order. Inclusion within its spacious boundaries, expulsion from them, had no such significance as have similar changes in a modern centralized state, with a developed, accentuated consciousness of its own, with intimate and compelling ties of patriotic and national feeling.

Within the loose framework of this empire, then, the feudal principle worked unchecked. It need occasion no surprise that the most feudal country in modern Europe is Germany. Feudal ideas and institutions, feudal principles and forces have, century after century, found in Central Europe their most favorable environment and opportunity. Their effects have proved perdurable.

We find feudalism in the other countries of Europe, in England, in France, in Spain. But we also find, what we do not find in the Holy Roman Empire, counteracting forces, seeking ascendancy and ultimately gaining it. And when they had gained it they stood forth as large and strongly centralized aggregations, as modern states. But this process of concentration did not occur in the Holy Roman German Empire, and largely because the innumerable princes were interested in preventing such a consummation. Their constant effort and ambition was to snatch from the Emperor some element of his power or influence and to add it to themselves. Thus, century after century, the process of nibbling went on and resulted, necessarily, in leaving a fragile shell, which Napoleon found little difficulty in dashing to pieces; outwardly a whited sepulchre, but within full of dead men's bones. The life of the

Empire was for many centuries merely a slow and ignoble process of decay.

As the princes of Germany were engaged, generation after generation, in mining and sapping the Empire, as they were using it as the medieval Romans used the Colosseum, as a quarry whence to filch their building material, as it was exposed to external attack on the part of foreigners who also had ambitions and could recognize an easy prey when they saw one, it was but natural and inevitable that outside parts should be lopped off, unless some regeneration or reinvigoration should occur, enabling the Empire to withstand the enemies that encompassed it without as well as those that swarmed within. But this regeneration never occurred, and the main reason why medieval Germany did not emerge in the modern period as a centralized and vigorous state, as did England and France and Spain, was because of the cupidity and the hostility of the German princes themselves. An accessory but distinctly secondary reason was the hostile environment in which it found itself.

Within the Holy Roman Empire were the regions that we know as Alsace and Lorraine. In the final break-up of the Carolingian monarchy these regions were lost to the kingdom that came to be known as

France and were drawn and held within the orbit of the German Empire. Not that the terms, Alsace and Lorraine, during those centuries signified at all what they signify to-day. The unity of Alsace, the unity of Lorraine, are of very recent origin. Alsace was at best a geographical expression, not a designation for a political entity, a state, except that there was for about a hundred years, in the seventh and eighth centuries, a duchy of Alsace which soon died, leaving no trace but the memory of a name. And not only were Alsace and Lorraine each lacking in the political and geographical unity which we associate with those designations to-day, but there was no connection between them. Each region went its own way, so to speak, each had its own history or rather its collection of many local histories. They did not live a common life, they did not follow the same law of evolution. For such diversity of experience the loose fabric of the Empire of which they formed a part was highly conducive, for the reasons which we have examined. Indeed that Empire was but another name for local independence, for the self-direction and self-control of hundreds of petty units.

Nowhere was the extreme *Zersplitterung*, as the Germans expressively call it, so characteristic of the

German map as a whole, better exemplified than in this very region which we call Alsace. Very numerous were the states lying there between the Vosges and the Rhine, very numerous the princes who claimed the right to rule or the suzerainty over this or that tiny or considerable parcel of territory. All the subtleties and complexities of the feudal régime were here operative to complete the confusion and disarray. One could not see the wood for the trees. The Hapsburg emperors possessed certain parts as family domains; the reigning princes of Wurtemberg, of the Palatinate, of Baden, of Lorraine, possessed certain parts. There were the ten free imperial cities, the famous Decapolis, Haguenau, Lindau, Rosheim, Munster, Colmar, Schlestadt, Wissembourg, Obernai, Kayserberg, Turkheim, jealous of their independence yet subject to the overlordship of the Emperor, his Landvogt or Prefect, each really a self-determining bourgeois republic. There were the republics of Strasburg and Mulhouse, the bishopric of Strasburg, lands dependent upon the bishop of Speyer, seignorial or ecclesiastical principalities galore, the seignory of Ribeaupierre, the barony of Fleckenstein, and many others. The history of Alsace for centuries is the history of innumerable struggles and wars between these insignificant principalities, and of wars into which they were drawn in various combinations by neighboring or outside states. Into this difficult chapter of history it is impossible, as it is unnecessary, for us to enter. We need only to grasp the general fact of ceaseless movement and agitation, of general insecurity, of the woful ravages of war with its recurrent devastation. We cannot here immerse ourselves in this tangled jungle of details. Generally neglected by the emperors busy in the east against Slavs, Hungarians, and Turks, lacking protection against others and against themselves, the Alsatians fought their ceaseless local wars, only rarely drawn into imperial or national currents of activity. At least their experience was a school of independence and self-reliance.

Lorraine, like Alsace, experienced the dissolving effects of the feudal system, although to a much less extent. The process of dividing and sub-dividing never went as far, and early experienced counteracting elements tending toward concentration. Its history is therefore much more simple. There were the Duchy of Lorraine and the Duchy of Bar, there were the counties, later bishoprics, of Metz, Toul, and Verdun, and lesser local entities, though never such a cloud of dust as floated over the river Ill. All these states were parts of the Empire but many of them were French in language and customs. Frequently connected by marriage or by military alliances or as feudal vassals with the kings of France, the Dukes of Lorraine fought side by side with the French at Crécy and other conflicts and made common cause with Joan of Arc against the English.

For century after century the numerous petty states of Alsace and Lorraine continued their internecine and local wars under the banner of the Empire. As border states, lying between the rest of the Empire and the compact and increasing mass of the French kingdom, they were exposed to opposite influences and to extra risks. Most of the Alsatians spoke German, the civilization of Alsace was prevailingly German, of Lorraine prevailingly French. Yet even Alsace showed French influences in her medieval literature, although it was written in German, and her best cathedral architects came from France, bringing with them their Gothic art and taste. The connection of Alsace and Lorraine with the Empire was as fragile as their rulers could make it, and have it exist at all. If there was one uniform law or practice in the history of the Holy Roman Empire it was this, that each of the three hundred and more states sought to achieve a maximum of independence of the Emperor, and succeeded. The Empire took on more and more the character of a name and an idea, losing more and more, as the centuries went by, the character of a nation.

France on the other hand, after long trials and tribulations, became a compact and vigorous state, increasingly self-conscious and ambitious. In any rivalry with the Empire, she possessed the manifest advantages of concentration of authority, and of greater prosperity, owing to her greater internal repose, the troublesome feudal elements having been tamed and curbed to an appreciable degree. France used her newly acquired unity and power for purposes of expansion.

The general conditions that prevailed in Germany aided her. But particularly did the new conditions created in the sixteenth century by the Protestant Reformation redound to her advantage. By playing a bold and skillful part in the religious wars which the Reformation precipitated, France added perceptibly to her stature. In part her annexations of territories which had hitherto been included within the Empire were natural and legitimate, were the payment for services rendered; in part they were the achievements of violence and usurpation.

The religious wars, which grew out of the clash of Protestantism and Catholicism, filled intermittently more than a century of European history, ending in the famous Treaty of Westphalia in 1648. They left the Empire conspicuously changed. This was particularly evident in the region whose history we are discussing, in Alsatian lands and in Lorraine.

The teachings of the Reformers early spread into various parts of Alsace, into Mulhouse, and the region round about, into Munster, particularly into Strasburg which, once having become Protestant, became a place of refuge for many Protestants of France during the periods of their persecution in that country. Religious and political questions became hopelessly intertwined. German Protestants supported the French Huguenots. Speaking very generally and mindful of numerous exceptions, it became the rule for Protestants in various countries to aid each other. They had a common enemy, the House of Austria, interested in the triumph of Catholicism, and in the secular might and power of the Hapsburg family, a family which ruled in Austria and in Spain.

With this family the House of Bourbon was inevitably, by the compelling force of circumstances, bound to clash. Hapsburg possessions surrounded France, in Spain, Italy, Germany, Belgium. Until France had pushed her boundaries back much farther from Paris than they were, no far-seeing French statesman could consider them secure. The great conflict between Bourbon and Hapsburg lay in the very nature of things. Its vicissitudes were to fill two centuries and more.

Alsace and Lorraine were inevitably involved in the *mêlée*. France was Catholic and her rulers intended that she should remain Catholic. But for nearly a hundred years she gave toleration to her Protestants, by the Edict of Nantes. And she gave more, not because of religious sympathy, but because of political hatred. The chief enemy of the Protestants was the Emperor, the House of Hapsburg. The chief enemy of France was also this self-same House. Under the circumstances it was entirely natural that the Protestants of Germany should seek the aid of France against the common enemy, Austria. This coalition of the small Protestant states of Germany, and of Sweden, Holland, and the Swiss, with France was the outstanding feature of the closing years of the Thirty Years War (1618–1648).

But nearly a century before that France had, in much the same way and by rendering somewhat the same service, begun to push her boundaries farther to the east. By the Treaty of Chambord, signed January, 1552, between Henry II of France and Maurice of Saxony and other Protestant princes of Germany it was agreed that, in return for services to be rendered to the Protestants in their death struggle with Charles V, Emperor of Germany, the bishoprics of Metz, Toul, and Verdun, officially parts of the Holy Roman Empire, should go to France. The service stipulated was rendered and France received her reward. Charles V made a tremendous effort in 1552 to recover Metz, but failed. From that time on, Metz, Toul, and Verdun have belonged to France, though that fact was not officially recognized until the signature of the Treaties of Westphalia in 1648.

The chief annexations, however, were gained by France as a result of her participation in the last phase of the Thirty Years War, more than eighty years later. Again her aid was required by the hard-pressed Protestants in their continuing and desperate struggle. With the coming of the Swedes in 1630, they were immensely reinforced and were for a while victorious. After the death of Gustavus Adolphus upon the field of battle came the ascendancy of the French as leaders in the general struggle against the religious and political absolutism of the Hapsburgs whose purpose was to destroy liberty of conscience throughout the Empire. This was the period of Louis XIII and Louis XIV, of Richelieu and Mazarin. In Alsace the Protestants, in order to defend themselves, appealed to France, inviting Louis XIII to occupy the fortified towns, which was done as early as 1633 and 1634. In 1635, France entered upon a war with the Emperor and the King of Spain and was victorious. The Peace of Westphalia, signed in 1648, brought the war to a close and it also introduced France into Alsace by giving her certain rights and possessions. These formed the "compensation" which the French received for the assistance which they had given during thirteen years of war to the enemies of the Emperor of Germany and the King of Spain.

The Emperor, by the Treaty of Westphalia, ceded to France, his rights and possessions in Alsace. But what was Alsace? As we have seen, it was not a unit but was a collection of independent states of different grades, personal and hereditary possessions of the Hapsburg family, independent free cities, baronies, and seigniories. The Emperor did not own these units but he did possess various rights of suzerainty over them, not as head of the House of Hapsburg, but as Emperor, the feudal overlord. Alsace, to repeat a point which must always be remembered, was not a united province with definite geographical boundaries. The Emperor's rights were of one kind in one part, of other kinds in other parts. It is a gross simplification of the transaction embedded in the Treaty of Westphalia to say that "the Empire ceded Alsace to France." What happened was far more complex, much more uncertain.

The provisions of that treaty were intentionally obscure and in some respects conflicting. What was explicitly given by one article seemed to be qualified or even contradicted by another article. Floods of ink have been spent in the hopeless attempt to explain the inexplicable, to elucidate that which defies elucidation. Into this disputatious maze of more than Alexandrian subtlety we cannot enter. No summary treatment would be useful, since it could not be adequate.

The Emperor, as head of the House of Hapsburg, ceded his hereditary possessions to France outright. These were mainly in southern Alsace, near Switzerland. This, according to the universal and unquestioned usage of the time, he had a right to do. In this region the title of France was clear, nor has it ever seriously been questioned. But this was only a small part of what came to be known as the province of Alsace.

The Emperor, as head of the House of Hapsburg, also had the right to exercise a sort of superior administration over the Ten Free Cities, which in the course of time had purchased of him the right of depending on him alone, that is, in practice, of being responsible to themselves alone, free from any obligations toward any nearer or more meddlesome ruler. This power was personified in the Emperor's representative, the Landvogt, or Prefect.

The Emperor also exercised simple feudal suzerainty over the other states, the seigniories, baronies, ecclesiastical or seigniorial principalities, which were crowded within the boundaries of what we know as Alsace.

Was the Emperor in ceding to France his rights in these two last categories of cases ceding territory or was he ceding only suzerainty and overlordship?

France showed in the years after 1648 that she considered she had practically acquired territory as well as sovereignty. Under the ambitious leadership of Louis XIV, anxious for aggrandizement, she pushed her interpretation of the treaty until in time she had actually incorporated all of what we know as Alsace into the French Kingdom. She was not precipitate but she was persistent. The famous "chambers of reunion" namely, certain French courts were ordered by the King of France to determine just what territories were properly included, in accordance with treaty provisions or feudal principles, in the regions now subject to the King. Their decisions were what it was expected they would be. The claims of the King were declared incontestable (1677-1680).

Thus virtually all of Alsace was brought directly under the control of France. Only Strasburg remained outside, a famous old imperial city. By an act of violence and in a time of peace Louis XIV seized Strasburg in September, 1681, and incorporated it in France, a deed which created an enormous sensation in Europe and which it is no purpose of ours to defend. The reader should keep in mind that it was an act no nobler and no more ignoble than innumerable previous acts of other monarchs, or than, in later times, the partition of Poland by Prussia, Austria, and Russia, or than the seizure of Silesia by Prussia or than the seizure of Schleswig-Holstein, Hanover, Frankfort, Hesse-Cassel, by Prussia, or of Alsace-Lorraine by Germany. German monarchs at least are estopped from criticising the ethics of the case, having themselves profited on a prodigiously vaster scale from the application of the same methods.

Thus by the legitimate results of the Treaties of Westphalia and by the illegitimate usurpations of Louis XIV during the thirty-three years subsequent to the signing of that treaty, Alsace had become materially subject in its entirety to France. Mulhouse, alone, was not included. This little, independent city, an Alsatian *enclave*, was connected with the Swiss cantons. Not until 1798 was it incorporated in France, when, for economic reasons, it voluntarily sought union with the greater republic.

Meanwhile, the territory which we know as Lorraine had had its own and a different history. Toul, Metz, Verdun, had, as we have seen, been drawn within the French orbit in 1552. The rest became in time an enlarged Duchy of Lorraine, feudal complications in Lorraine being fewer and less intricate than those in Alsace. This Duchy had early become practically, through the payment of a fixed sum of money, independent of the Empire—was *liber et non incorporalibus*. In 1736 it was given to Stanislaus Leszcynski, the dethroned King of Poland, on condition that at his death it should pass to the crown of France. Stanislaus was father-in-law to Louis XV, and his chief pleasure, as monarch *ad interim*, was to make Nancy, his capital, resemble Versailles as nearly as he could on a limited income. Under the influence of his taste, which was thoroughly French, Nancy became a spacious and luxurious city. Lorraine was largely French in language, French in its interests and connections, and the administrative system used by Stanislaus in the government of his peaceful state was French in character.

When Stanislaus died in 1766, Lorraine became French. The process of assimilation had already been completed. No pear ever fell to the ground more naturally, more quietly, at its moment of complete maturity.

Such then is the varied history of the annexation of Alsace and Lorraine to France, a history running through nearly two centuries and a half, from the acquisition of Metz in 1552 to that of Mulhouse in 1798. Considering the ideas, usages, and practices of the times, this history was entirely normal. As compensation for distinct and valuable services rendered, by family inheritance, and by acts of violence and usurpation, France had acquired these famous territories which were destined to an even greater, if more melancholy, fame in our own day.

What use did she make of her acquisitions? A

very wise use, in striking contrast to that made by Germany after 1871. Unlike some modern rulers, the Grand Monarch, whose powers were absolute, did not undertake to overthrow the entire preceding régime, and to Gallicise quickly and by methods more or less violent the daily life and even the mental outlook of his new subjects. On the contrary, the intention and the practice of the government was to disturb as little and as inconspicuously as possible the usages and traditions of the country. The ancient territorial divisions were respected and Alsace continued to show, as before, a multitude of local sovereignties, lay and ecclesiastical. Only, in the hierarchy, the King of France stood where formerly the Emperor had stood. The old administrative machinery was allowed to continue largely as before. The traditions of the land were respected. No attempt was made to force the Alsatians to use the French language. No military service was required of them.

The result of this wise policy was to create the felicitous impression among the people concerned, that nothing or almost nothing was changed. Friction was thus avoided. Life moved along normally and in the same old grooves. The new régime could strike roots, slowly it is true, but all the more solidly. No racial opposition was aroused. Changes were effected, but so gradually and so beneficently that only the advantages of the new connection were apparent. The higher administrative system of France, represented by the intendant, was introduced, but the local administrators were largely the old seigneurs of the numerous divisions which gave to the map of Alsace so bizarre an appearance. Those petty feudal sovereigns continued to appoint their bailiffs, who were charged with collecting the taxes, with supervising the village officials, with the enforcement of local justice. The result was that the peasant in the little village saw no change in his situation and was unconscious of the fact that he had ceased to be a subject of Ferdinand of Hapsburg and was now a subject of Louis XIV.

He saw, in time, that he was being treated somewhat more justly, for one of the changes that the French gradually introduced was the revision, through a superior royal court, of the unjust or burdensome decisions of the petty seigniorial courts. Also, now that she formed a part of a large and strong state, Alsace was no longer almost continuously ravaged by wars as she had been. The eighteenth century presented a great contrast to the seventeenth in this respect. The King of France could give, and did give, far greater protection to his subjects than the Emperor of Germany had ever given. An increasing prosperity was the natural consequence of this greater security. The hideous devastations of the Thirty Years Wars were rapidly repaired.

This golden age did not continue unclouded, but in the main it did continue down to the French Revolution. The demoralization and extravagance of the state during the long and fatal reign of Louis XV had inevitably their unfavorable reaction upon Alsace, as upon the rest of France. During all this period, however, a natural and healthy process of assimilation went on, unforced. The diffusion of the French language, "the King's language" as it was called, was aided by the constantly increasing number of officials, civil, military, ecclesiastical, sent into the province for various purposes. The local nobility and many of the bourgeoisie saw the advantage of learning it. But for all internal matters German remained the official language employed by the administrative agents down to 1789. This result of the gradual spread of a knowledge of French was all the more satisfactory, as it was not obtained by political pressure and propaganda. The House of Bourbon, from the

Treaty of Westphalia to the French Revolution, never thought of preventing or hampering the use of German in Alsace, never considered its suppression necessary as a means of hastening the assimilation of the province.

The eighteenth century was to witness a sweeping transformation, an extraordinary reinvigoration of the life of this peaceful province. At the beginning of that century Alsatian society presented the same distinctive characteristics it had long presented. It was a specimen of old feudal Germany. A few changes only had occurred. The *fleur-de-lis* floated over Alsatian towns and fortresses where formerly the double-headed Austrian eagle had been seen. French *louis d'or* circulated in the haunts of trade. At the end of that century, however, Alsatian society was radically, fundamentally, permanently altered, in structure and in spirit, in organization, in ideas, in emotions, in institutions, in political convictions. A movement of ideas, a process of assimilation, a period of incubation, at first slow and almost imperceptible, was, toward the middle of the eighteenth century, hastened by fructifying impulses from without and swept on to complete fruition in the general passion and commotion of the final decade. This small section of medieval Germany was changed into a highly modern organism, instinct with energy, with an outlook upon life that no more resembled its former outlook than the steam engine resembles the spinning wheel. Alsace and Lorraine were almost literally born again.

The first results of the contact of Alsace and Lorraine with France were, as we have seen, longer periods of peace, greater personal security and consequently greater prosperity, a better administration, a larger measure of justice. The more sweeping changes, just alluded to, occurred as a result of changes which took place in France itself. A whole new world of ideas was rapidly and brilliantly expounded by the so-called philosophers of the eighteenth century. The new spirit expressed by thinkers, poets, and pamphleteers was marvellously contagious and was contagious because it was so optimistic, so bold and fresh and human. This new and passionate philosophy was highly critical of men's institutions, destructive of their traditions, of their ways of thinking and of feeling. Pointing out unsparingly the abuses of society, the hoary, benumbing restrictions laid upon men by the dead hand of the past, the writers of the eighteenth century urged innumerable changes. The past hung lightly upon these reformers. The future was what interested them, a future fairer far, because more rational and more altruistic, than anything that history could show. Destructive, constructive, fundamentally sound and partially fanciful, the new philosophy expressed admirably the longing and the aspiration of a new age toward whose realization it powerfully contributed.

The writings of Montesquieu, Voltaire, Rousseau and others stirred the intellectual world of France and, to a lesser degree, of other countries. This critical spirit of the eighteenth century, this ferment of a coming revolution, filtered into Alsatian society too, into the upper classes first, then into the middle, then even into the lower. Some of the new liberal ideas were eminently of a character to appeal to the peasantry, to the masses, if they should hear of them. Thus what had been lacking at first in the contact of France and her new provinces, the principle of spiritual cohesion, was being supplied by this growing community of new ideas, ideas of reform, political, social, and economic.

When the final crisis of this great century occurred, when action succeeded thought, when revolution succeeded philosophy, the people of Alsace and Lorraine were among the most eager to salute the new day, with its gospel of liberty, equality, and fraternity. The Bourbon monarchy, by its intelligent and tactful treatment of them from the moment of their annexation, by wisely trusting to the knitting of interests and affections that would come with the lapse of time, had performed a useful work and had been rewarded with unmistakable evidences of contentment and even gratitude. The new régime, which was now to supplant the old, aroused enthusiasm.

Alsace had never been represented in a meeting of the States-General, as none had been held since she had been annexed to France. Now, in 1789, she was called upon to elect twenty-four representatives to the assembly which was quickly to become so memorable, six nobles, six ecclesiastics, and twelve members of the third estate. Among the last was Reubell who was to play a conspicuous part in the Revolution and was ultimately to be one of the five Directors who were to constitute the executive of France. With these elections to the States-General began a far more intimate and pervasive connection with France than Alsace had ever before known. From that time on to 1871, Alsace was not only in body but in soul as truly a part of France as any section of the country. The large majority of her people spoke German, but they thought and fought as Frenchmen, and, in the fervor of their passion, the completeness of their immersion in French politics and wars, it is impossible to discover any sense on their part of their being a peculiar people, or even the most remote indication that they regarded themselves as an alien population, a people in captivity. There was a singular contrast between the external aspect of the country which resembled Germany, and the warm, instinctive, unquestioning attachment of its inhabitants to France. The peasantry were thoroughly French in feeling, grateful to the monarchy for frequently protecting them from the injustice of their immediate suzerains. The bourgeoisie profited from the connection with a great and relatively progressive country. The writers, thinkers, and professional classes looked toward Paris as the fountain head of intellectual life.

Alsace, like France in general, was a land of the Old Régime. Like France, too, it emerged out of the hot tumult of the times, a land of the New Régime. The struggles, incidents, vicissitudes of this rapid and radical change were the same as in the country as a whole. It was, as everyone knows, not a peaceful and orderly evolution of a new form of society out of an old. It was a violent convulsion, a consuming flame, destructive of the established order. By sweeping the ground quite clear, it allowed the new ideas and principles of the eighteenth century a field for experimentation in the work of construction of a new system of society.

This significant and stirring history cannot be summarized, either here or elsewhere. It must be studied in detail by anyone who wishes to understand its multifarious phenomena.

Suffice it to say that the course of the French Revolution was the same in this corner of France as it was elsewhere. We find the same complications, the same oppositions of social classes, the same warfare of parties, the same mounting frenzy of internecine conflicts, the same increasing radicalism and ruthlessness. Alsatian society was torn by the same furious dissensions as was that of Normandy or Provence. This epic conflict, a conflict between the Old Régime and the new aspirations of the nation, was enacted in every section, literally in every nook and corner of France. The local life of every province and every hamlet was but a cross-section of the national life as a whole. The partisans of things as they were clashed in angry and finally in fratricidal warfare with the partisans of reform. Their relative strength varied more or less according to the region but the contest and the agitation were everywhere fundamentally identical. To tell the story of the Revolution in Alsace one would be obliged to tell its story in France. Alsace was but a microcosm, France the macrocosm. Influences that radiated from Paris were felt to the farthest confines of the land. Influences from the provinces converged upon Paris and determined the actions of the central government. This reciprocal interplay of forces went on unceasingly, the impetus increasing with every passing month. Alsace had her municipal revolutions, her popularly improvised national guards, her war upon the châteaux, her festivals of federation, her Jacobin clubs, her revolutionary tribunals, her guillotine. An immense Phrygian cap was for years to be seen on the top of the spire of the Strasburg Cathedral—symbol of the Revolution, thus visible from afar. In June, 1790, Strasburg celebrated with great enthusiasm the victory over feudalism and the Old Régime. The national guards marched to the middle of the bridge which spanned the Rhine, and planted there a tricolor flag bearing the inscription "Here begins the Land of Liberty." The *Marseillaise* was composed in Strasburg by Rouget de Lisle who happened to be residing there, and was first sung at a dinner given by the Revolutionary mayor, Dietrich. In the meetings of the clubs the burning questions of the day were passionately discussed in both the languages of the province—French and German. The unenfranchised of the communes rose against the municipal governments, the Magistrates, the patrician monopolizers of local power, overthrew them, and installed themselves. The peasants rose against their overlords, ecclesiastical and lay, destroyed the evidences of their subjection to them, and eagerly bought or seized their lands, when these were confiscated by the state and sold. Thus the peasantry became committed to the new régime by the most evident self-interest. The decrees of August 4th were hailed with joy by the mass of the Alsatian people, as by the general mass of their countrymen. The citizens of Strasburg, assembled in the public square in March, 1790, drew up a solemn address to the National Assembly which contained this phrase: "To this spot, where our fathers gave themselves regretfully to France, we have come to cement by our oaths our union with her. We have sworn and we swear again to shed even the last drop of our blood to maintain the constitution. If the city of Strasburg has not had the glory of herself giving the first example to the cities of the realm she will at least enjoy that of being, by the energy of the patriotism of her inhabitants, one of the most powerful of the bulwarks of French liberty."

The religious legislation of the French assemblies, or rather the legislation affecting the Church, made enthusiastic friends and bitter enemies in Alsace as elsewhere and in many instances those who were friends at first were rendered hostile as the policy developed. The peasants were glad enough to be freed from the tithes and the feudal dues which they had hitherto had to pay to the ecclesiastical authorities and foundations which were particularly numerous among them. They were glad enough of the opportunity to buy church lands, as were the bourgeoisie also, many of whom now became landowners of importance during this period of extensive transference of real estate. There had existed in Alsace more than a hundred monastic institutions, many of them richly endowed with lands and with other forms of wealth. Those into whose hands they now passed were disinclined to relinquish them. But with the passage by the Constituent Assembly of the Civil Constitution of the Clergy a cross-current set in, and the leaders of the counter-revolution now had a handle with which to stir up civil dissension. The Duke de Rohan, the "Necklace Cardinal," the chief ecclesiastical dignitary of Alsace, who had left his palace in Strasburg and withdrawn across the Rhine to Ettenheim in Baden, led the counter-revolution, with genuine ecclesiastical finesse and subtlety. The result was that Alsace became the hotbed of intrigue and of disaffection, which was met by more and more vigorous legislation from Paris. The land was torn by religious convulsions which added their peculiar fury to the already overcharged distractions of the time. "Martyr" priests and their supporters consequently felt the full, fell wrath of the politicians who proceeded, under the pressure of the elusive conflict, from one excess to another. Strasburg saw her cathedral turned into a Temple of Reason, a hint that was followed in many other Alsatian towns. A fierce decree of the period of the Terror ordered the destruction of the innumerable statues that clustered over the portals and on the façade of the famous church, a decree only partially carried out, owing to the disobedient connivance of the local authorities.

Thus the internecine struggles went on between revolutionaries and reactionaries, between conservatives and radicals, between "aristocrats" and "Jacobins," fanned by every breeze that blew to a scorching, consuming flame.

The great Revolutionary Wars, which began in 1792, and which subsequently merged into the Napoleonic wars and did not end till Waterloo twenty-three years later, wars which twisted the Revolution out of all resemblance to its early promise and sadly deformed it in every way, grew, in part, out of a problem peculiar to Alsace, a problem the product of her singular history.

Among the numerous feudal fiefs which diversified the political map of Alsace before 1789, making it a strange patchwork, were many which belonged to German princes. These princes had sworn fealty to their overlord, the King of France, yet they exercised a power over scores of thousands of Alsatians which intimately affected their daily lives. The Landgrave of Hesse-Darmstadt had very extensive possessions in Alsace; the Duke of Württemberg, the Duke of Zweibrücken, the Bishop of Speyer, and others were the immediate sovereigns of larger or smaller territories. A sixth of the soil of the province thus belonged to foreigners, who, though lieges of the French king, yet sent bailiffs and judges from beyond the Rhine to exact taxes and administer justice and to perform other acts of government in these territories. They did this, of course, in the German way, and thus, for most practical purposes, a part of France was really ruled from Germany. This fact illustrates one of those confusing, crisscross relationships so characteristic of the feudal system.

The proclamation of the principles of 1789, particularly that of the equality of all Frenchmen before the law, was a direct challenge to this system, and when the decrees of August 4 were passed there was a general protest of these German princes and they considered that the moment was opportune for them to lay their grievances before the Diet of the German Empire, and to solicit the support of the Emperor, Leopold II, who willingly posed as their defender. This difficulty, which did not yield to diplomatic adjustment, was one of the causes of the war which was officially declared April 20, 1792. One result of the Revolution was the complete elimination of these German princes, of this foreign influence in Alsace. During the debates in the Constituent Assembly on this contentious matter the great lawyer, Merlin of Douai, declared that from the point of view of the new public law the complaint of the German princes was unjustifiable and untenable: "The people of Alsace have united themselves with the people of France because they have wished to; it is their will alone, and not the Treaty of Westphalia, which has legalized this union, and, as they have never attached any condition relative to these princely fiefs, no indemnity can be claimed." In the end neither the German princes nor the native Alsatian nobles received any compensation for the privileges they had long enjoyed, and, also, long abused.

Thus was accomplished a further liberation of the soil. The Franco-German system which applied to a sixth of the territory of Alsace was irremediably destroyed.

In the same year that the Revolutionary Wars began, the Bourbon monarchy was overthrown and the Republic was proclaimed. A new and momentous phase of French history began, from which modern France and modern Europe have never been able to shake themselves permanently free. A new society was developed, Modern France, which, despite various vicissitudes, has gone on developing ever since. With this profound and sweeping transformation Alsace and Lorraine were intimately associated at every step. In the tremendous and desperate wars, as in the fierce political and social struggles within, Alsace participated with all her energy, and all her soul. There was no holding aloof, no separate or individual action. There was the most complete absorption in the activities of the nation as a whole. Alsatian life did not flow in channels of its own; the local stream merged into the general current that swept France onward to her strange new destinies, and all sense of a distinct and different personality was utterly dissipated. At the beginning of the Revolution, Alsace was still, from many points of view, an alien in the French family. But now the fusion was completed in the immense heat of the boiling furnace which we call the French Revolution. The Revolution, by methods that were sometimes violent, but particularly by the contagious influence of its principles of freedom, by the generosity of its appeal to the instinctive love of liberty, easily captivated the Alsatian people, who, with all their traditional attachments to liberal ideas, born of their long experience of semi-independence within the loose fabric of the Holy Roman Empire, were willing converts to radical republicanism and democracy.

Service in the Revolutionary wars completed the process of assimilation. The sons of Alsace and Lorraine flocked into the volunteer armies, and some of them became famous generals, like Kellermann and Kléber. Their achievements and their fame only intensified the fervor of their patriotic provinces and acted upon their fellow citizens as a powerful incitement to imitation and emulation. As Rodolphe Reuss, a native of Alsace and her historian has said: "Considered as a whole, the Revolution exerted a profound and durable influence upon the generations of that day and of the days to come; the impress which Alsace received from this memorable epoch differentiates still, after forty years of annexation, the inhabitants of its cities, big and little, the Alsatian peasants and workingmen, from the peasants and the bourgeois across the Rhine. And the reason is that they were liberated by the Revolution from the yoke of monarchical superstition; that they have preserved the memory, more or less definite, the impression more or less keen, but ineffaceable, of that collection of lofty doctrines, of aspirations for brotherhood, of visions of the future which are summarized in the phrases, 'the principles of '89.' Those who breathed that air were never to forget it."

The distinguished French historian, Fustel de Coulanges, at one time a professor in the University of Strasburg, where he gave the famous course of lectures which were perpetuated in the *Cité antique*, a remarkable picture of the life of the ancient world, in a letter addressed to Theodore Mommsen in the year 1870, described the situation with undeniable accuracy when he said, "Do you know what made Alsace French? It was not Louis XIV, it was our Revolution of 1789. Since that moment Alsace has followed all our destinies, she has lived our life. All that we think, she thinks, all that we feel, she feels. She has shared our victories and our defeats, our glory and our mistakes, all our joy, and all our sorrow."

The Napoleonic period continued the work of consolidation and inner fusion. Since the 18th of Brumaire there has been, properly speaking, no history of Alsace. Alsace and Lorraine were swallowed up, like all the other provinces of old France, in the general history of the country. Napoleon cut short the political education of Alsace and Lorraine and France in democracy and republicanism, putting obedience to a single mind, itself a leveller, in its place. But he continued the work of the Revolution in some respects, in binding more and more closely together all the peoples of his empire in the collective work of the nation, and particularly in war; continuing, expanding, intensifying, in this sphere, the activities of the Republic. By the Concordat, Napoleon brought religious peace to these essentially religious provinces. By his scientific and orderly administrative system, with its prefects and subprefects, he held the whole population tightly in the mesh of centralized power, and emphasized the might of the state; and by maintaining the social reforms of the Revolution intact he held the peasantry in the hollow of his hand.

But Napoleon's particular specialty was fighting, and in that long series of glorious and of catastrophic wars, which fill this dynamic and thrilling period, Alsace and Lorraine took an honorable, wholehearted and distinguished part, showing by act and attitude that they were French in every fibre and to the very marrow of their bones. To talk of these people being Germans because their language was German was sheer and jejune nonsense. By every token a people can give they were completely and proudly French.

On the Arc de Triomphe in Paris are inscribed the names of twenty-eight Alsatian generals. The careers and characters of these men were the common talk of the Alsatian fireside and of the camp. They illustrated the democracy of the French army. Every Alsatian soldier knew that, if he had talent, he could have a similar career. The door of opportunity was wide open. No privileged noble class monopolized officers' positions. No questions were asked about one's origin, only about one's ability and achievement. To these brilliant names every raw recruit knew that he might add his own. If there was a will there might be a way.

The quality of many of these outstanding figures, the glory of their provinces, lay not in their blood, but in their deeds. They were the homely heroes of democracy, speaking the authentic language of the people. Thus, Lefebvre, a popular hero who never blushed for the modesty of his origin, said to a pretentious nobleman, "Don't be so proud of your ancestors; I am an ancestor, myself." He, the son of a miller, and his wife, a former servant in a country inn, were no parvenus, inasmuch as they were entirely unaffected by the brilliancy of their new position in life, and maintained unchanged their simple dignity, their native wit, and their picturesque way of talking.

Or take this remark of Kléber, a typical Alsatian, direct, plain, often headstrong, who kept his habit of speaking his mind bluntly even to General Bonaparte when others lost the habit; "Riches I do not want. A single farthing more, and particularly if acquired in some bad way, would derange the entire system of my happiness and my philosophy." And again, in a letter to the Directory when offered the position of commander-in-chief, Kléber said: "My first counsellor, whose censure I am most afraid of, is the feeling of my own powers, is my conscience. It commands me not to compromise the interests of the Republic by accepting a post beyond my ability."

Not only Kellermann and Kléber of Strasburg, not only Lefebvre of Rouffach, not only Rapp, the hero of Austerlitz and Essling, wounded twenty-four times, faithful but frank, blaming the divorce of Josephine, advising against the Russian campaign, but also many others, Marshal Ney of Saarlouis, Custine and Richepanse of Metz, and General Schramm, who began life as a tender of geese, all added imperishable lustre to the history of Alsace and Lorraine, their native lands. Count de Ségur was quite right when he said in his *Memoirs* that there were "no better, no more generous, no braver Frenchmen in all France."

When this Napoleonic epic was over, when its doom was signed and sealed at Waterloo, the people of Alsace and Lorraine who had contested, though in vain, every inch of their territory with the oncoming invader, who had shared in the grandeur of the period, who had fought magnificently for the common cause, were called upon to pay the price of defeat. The second Treaty of Paris, of November 20, 1815, began the dismemberment of France, and at the expense of Alsace and Lorraine. Alsace lost territory in the north, including the strong fortress of Landau which for four centuries had been one of the ten free cities, the Decapolis. Lorraine lost Saarlouis and the valuable iron mines of the Saar, Prussia thus beginning the process of acquiring French iron deposits which she was to carry much farther in 1871, and to endeavor to complete in the war that began in 1914.

Prussia demanded all of Alsace, as did also Bavaria; and also demanded parts of Lorraine. The German desire for French territory was very strong in 1814 and 1815, and was expressed in Moritz Arndt's pamphlet on "The Rhine, a German River but not the Boundary of Germany." But the victorious Allies did not accede to these demands, nor to the other demand, voiced by another poet, that the "enchained Alsatians" should be released from the "infernal" yoke to which, it was asserted, they were subject. Alsace and Lorraine were left substantially intact to France, to which they belonged by every desire of their people, by every tie that binds. Even the more intelligent Germans recognized the real sentiments of these "brothers." The *Rheinischer Merkur*, an important liberal nationalist paper of that day, admitted that the Alsatians had talked, if their country were handed over, of emigrating with their cattle, after having set fire to their villages, and the editor explained this grim, defiant resolution as owing to the fear the Alsatians had of being enslaved to selfish petty despots, as were the people across the Rhine. The poet Rickert wrote a "Song of Shame" expressing the wrath of the German soldiers at being forced to leave the soil of France: "And you, Alsace, race degermanized, you also mock, O final shame!"

To this outburst of German ambition, a Strasburg poet Stoeber replied, using the native dialect which he loved and saying that while his "lyre was German, his sword was French and faithful to the Gallic cock." The Alsatians, he added, were not hybrids; they were Frenchmen, although interested in the language, the literature, the achievements of Germany. Stoeber disavowed Napoleon's wars of conquest. "But if it is a question of the wars of the Revolution in which we fought for our independence and for the preservation of the imprescriptible rights of man, we are proud of our zeal," he said, and he closed with the eirenic hope that there would be a reconciliation of "the strength of Hermann and the courage of Roland."

Many years later a German historian, writing after 1870, admitted that in 1815 in Alsace and Lorraine there was to be found no trace of the ancient racial fellowship with the German brothers.

Three years after Waterloo the people of Alsace and Lorraine knew these brothers better and liked them even less for, from 1815 to 1818, the Allied armies occupied those regions until the last indemnity, exacted by the Treaty of Paris, was paid. The impression they left behind them with the rural and urban population was anything but agreeable.

From the fall of Napoleon in 1815 to the Franco-German war in 1870, Alsace and Lorraine lived the same life that all the other parts of France lived, pursuing the comparatively even tenor of their ways, prosperous and contented. Reinvigorated by the extraordinary energies which had been aroused and stimulated by the Revolution, their outlook broadened and deepened by the sweep and might of the Napoleonic era, freed from the last remnants of feudalism, and endowed with the new democratic institutions and ideas which survived the overthrow of the Napoleonic régime, imbued with the principles of '89 which they found congenial to their temperament, Alsace and Lorraine engaged, henceforth, in all the activities of the most modern state of Europe and experienced all the vicissitudes of the reigns of Louis XVIII, Charles X, Louis Phillipe, of the Second Republic and of the Second Empire. In politics they were usually to be found on the liberal side, sympathetic to the revolutions of 1830 and 1848. General Foy, one of the great parliamentary leaders of the Liberals of the period of the Restoration, was so impressed with the democratic tone of Alsatian society that after a voyage through that country in 1821 he exclaimed, "If ever the love of what is great and generous should grow weak in the hearts of the people of old France, her people should cross the Vosges and visit Alsace, there to renew their patriotism and their energy."

This liberal spirit was maintained and strengthened in Alsace by the spectacle of crass reaction and of persecution which spread over Germany during the era of Metternich, and particularly after the odious Carlsbad Decrees were put in force, gagging the German people. These persecutions were frequent after 1815 and resulted in the expulsion or flight from Germany of almost all the intellectuals, journalists, students, authors, publishers. A large number of these found a refuge in Strasburg. Polish refugees came too, and enjoyed the same safety and hospitality. Association with the fugitives from despotism only confirmed the attachment of the native population to the freedom that was theirs.

In 1840 was inaugurated the monument to Kléber in Strasburg in the square which bears his name. Beneath it lies the body of the great general, the hero of Alsace, and his resting place has been the shrine of patriotic pilgrimages from that day to this. In 1842, occurred the celebrations in honor of Gutenberg, the inventor of printing, the inauguration of his statue by David d'Angers, the opening of an exposition of typography, all of which festivities moved and stirred the local pride. In 1848, Alsace observed with great enthusiasm the two hundredth anniversary of the annexation to France. On this occasion the Mayor of Strasburg, addressing his compatriots, said: "Surely we no longer need to make a solemn and public profession of our inviolable attachment to France. France does not doubt us, she has confidence in Alsace. But if Germany still cherishes chimerical illusions, if she thinks that the persistence of the German tongue in our countryside and cities is a sign of irresistible sympathy and attraction toward her, let her undeceive herself. Alsace is just as French as Brittany, Flanders, the country of the Basques—and she wishes to remain so."

This utterance, like many others which might be quoted, was no doubt intended as a reply to numerous recurrent expressions of German aspiration to "recover" Alsace and Lorraine, which threw an increasing shadow over the future. The fundamental hatred of the Germans for the French flamed up from time to time. But it inspired no serious alarm in Alsace, so firm and natural did her position seem. Moreover, in 1848 it seemed for a time likely that Germany herself might become free and democratic, and that any menace that might exist in the recollections of the German people would then be dissipated. A free country would respect the freedom of its neighbors.

But that chance for the harmony which would come from unity of ideas and principles and feelings was soon dissipated. The great liberal movement of Germany in 1848 was short-lived and triumphant reaction was soon installed in Vienna and Berlin. An odious period of repression and persecution ensued, teaching the new generation the lesson their fathers had learned from Metternich and Frederick William III, that Germany was feudal, monarchical, unfree, and that her governing classes intended she should remain so. The evolution of Germany was not to be conducted by her democrats, but by her aristocrats, who proclaimed, through their authoritative spokesman, Otto von Bismarck, the efficacy and the virility of the good old method of rule by "blood and iron." The rise of Prussia, the easy and momentous victories of 1864 in the Danish War, of 1866 in the war with Austria, and the successful reënthronement of force in the political life of Germany were well calculated to inspire alarm and apprehension. And nowhere did they inspire more alarm and apprehension than in Alsace. Men who were attentive to the signs of the times observed the ominous growth of an ardent chauvinism beyond the Rhine. This boded nothing good for the Alsatians and many of them knew it. After 1866, the German menace became dangerous, and when in 1870, the war between Prussia and France broke out, engineered by the cold Machiavellianism of Bismarck, exploiting the folly of Napoleon III, the heart of the Alsatians sank within them, as they were fully alive to the meaning it might have for them. They knew the minute and careful preparation of the enemy, the criminal insouciance of the government of France.

But they rose as one man, in a magnificent *élan* of patriotism, to defend their country and their hearths. The record of the Alsatians and Lorrainers in the Franco-German War, their eagerness to give the last full measure of devotion, is a sufficient comment upon the German assertion that they were Germans, brothers in captivity, yearning for release, an assertion for which no shred of proof has ever been given and which flies in the face of evidence that is overwhelming. The Alsatians and Lorrainers fought the invader tooth and nail, reddening their native lands with their life blood in the hope that these might remain the lands of the free as well as of the brave. Many of the famous battle-fields of this calamitous war lay on the soil of Alsace and Lorraine, Wissembourg, Wörth, Spicheren, Borny, Mars-la-Tour, and Gravelotte. Crushed by overwhelming forces, the two provinces were nearly conquered. Only Strasburg and Metz held out.

Strasburg was completely surrounded on August 12th. On the 13th the first shells began to fall. Two days later the real bombardment began and was directed, not against the fortifications, but against the public and private buildings in the heart of the city, against women and children. On the 18th a private school was struck, five little girls were killed outright, six others frightfully mutilated. The system adopted by the German commander, von Werder, whom the Strasburgers called Mörder (assassin), was that of so terrorizing the inhabitants that they would bring irresistible pressure upon the French commander to surrender, a method which we of to-day are in a position to understand. Werder refrained from nothing that might inspire terror. The people took refuge in their cellars and when their houses caught fire and they emerged in order to try to extinguish the flames they were unable to do so since the enemy made the blazing houses the target of concentrated attack in order to prevent this very thing. On August 24th and 25th, one of the great churches, the *Temple Neuf* went up in flames; also the art museum, and two public libraries with all their treasures, including many precious manuscripts invaluable for the history of Strasburg and Alsace. On the 26th the roof of the Cathedral took fire, its tiles of copper melting in bluish flames, while projectiles demolished much of the wonderful stone carving of the building and broke the windows of stained glass, the glory of the Middle Ages.

This policy of terrorization, of more than primal barbarism, did not terrify, but only steeled the resolution of the citizens and filled them with an abiding hatred of their enemies. Their commander said in a proclamation to the people whose priceless possessions were being blown to pieces or burned to cinders, "Your heroism, at this hour, lies in patience." The national legislature in Paris passed a resolution, August 31st, to the effect that "Strasburg has deserved well of the Fatherland." These two utterances were not exaggerations but were rather understatements.

The odious work continued, the Palace of Justice, the railroad station, the church attached to the municipal hospital, the theatre, the prefecture and other public buildings were demolished in turn— ruins everywhere. The long agony finally drew to a close. On September 27 the white flag was hoisted on the Cathedral and on the 28th an immense concourse of citizens witnessed the departure of their defenders into captivity. Cries of *Vive la France* broke from the sobbing, stricken multitude.

Such was the début of Germany as the ruler of Alsace. The memories aroused by the bombardment of Strasburg have never been forgotten. During the siege, three hundred civilians, men, women, and children were killed, and more than two thousand wounded. More than 200,000 projectiles had been hurled against the city, over six hundred houses had been burned. Such was the first manifestation of the love of the Germans for their long lost brothers. What caused the greatest indignation among the people of Strasburg was the fury shown in the destruction of their public buildings and particularly their cathedral, which was not damaged accidentally but intentionally, and without military justification.

CHAPTER III

WHY GERMANY ANNEXED ALSACE-LORRAINE

"LET us take, after that we shall always find lawyers enough to defend our rights," said Frederick the Great, with his customary frankness and cynicism. Frederick is the greatest national hero of Germany.

But in the case of Alsace-Lorraine the procedure followed was not quite that used in the seizure of Silesia. In this instance jurists, professors, editors, statesmen, warriors, even scientists were prolific in finding reasons for the act before it was committed, and they have been prolific since, despite the official dictum that since 1871 there has been nothing to discuss.

Let us examine these German apologetics for this famous achievement.

Ethnology has been invoked, and that too in no intentional spirit of humor or persiflage. Skulls found in the gravel deposits of Alsace and Lorraine are of the German type, dolichocephalic. Considering the number of invasions from the east to the west which these regions have experienced in the course of the ages, we must admit the fact. In the resolve to show ourselves true scholars, lovers of a somewhat dubious science, we must also note the fact that in the excavations Celtic reminders, brachycephalic in character, are also abundantly discovered. All of which proves, we take it, one well-attested fact of history, that the Germans have frequently emigrated into Alsace, interposing themselves among the primitive peoples. In this mensuration of skulls honors are easy, and commingled, and of doubtful pertinence. One reflection occurs to the inquiring mind. If modern states are to be ethnographic unities, if racial lines are to determine national boundaries, why should not Germany incorporate Livonia and the city of Riga? Why should not Prussia incorporate Holland, why should not France annex Belgium, why should not Spain take Portugal? Again, why should there not be two or three Switzerlands, several Russias, a half a dozen Austrias? Why should not Scotland be separated from England? It should be also noted that the Prussians have shown no conspicuous signs of a willingness to give up their Polish possessions out of respect for ethnology. Evidently, in their opinion, there are limits to the applicability of its saving grace. One thing is certain and that is that if the political map of Europe is to be redrawn along racial lines the world will see some very remarkable changes and will experience several severe shocks.

But the Germans have other arrows in their quiver. One is barbed with a linguistic theory. Alsace and Lorraine were retaken, we are told, because their people speak the German language, and because, therefore, their affinity is with Germany. A good many superficial people have been impressed with this argument. It is worth examining. If those who speak a given language are therefore justified in annexing others who speak it, even if the latter do not wish to be annexed, if the boundaries of the state are to extend as far as the boundaries of the language, then, necessarily, per contra, they are to extend no farther, for each language presumably has the same rights as every other. If this standard of measurement is to be applied to the modern world, we must again be prepared for surprises.

For this principle of one language one people, is loaded with dynamite. In France, even within her present boundaries, more than one language is spoken. Are the Bretons, are the Basques, therefore, to be cut off, as Alsace-Lorraine was cut off?

In Switzerland, three languages are spoken, and indeed even a fourth. Would Germany, therefore, be justified in annexing the larger part of Switzerland, France a smaller part, even Italy a section? But the national feeling, and the common patriotism of the Swiss are as deep-seated as are those of Germany, are rooted solidly in the history of several centuries, and the Swiss would, it is entirely safe to say, defend their country, if attacked, as unanimously and as fiercely as the Germans theirs. Swiss history is there to indicate what would assuredly happen if this much trumpeted linguistic theory should prompt aggression from neighbors who speak the languages spoken in the proud and sturdy Alpine state.

Again, the people of the United States speak English; nevertheless they were content to separate from England. Would they give enthusiastic support to the theory of language, should England attempt to apply it?

But what is sauce for the goose ought to be, also, sauce for the gander. If this linguistic criterion or norm is to be applied, it must, out of regard for the most elementary logic, be applied consistently. Prussia's devotion to the doctrine leaves something to be desired. The theory we are discussing, would, for instance, hardly justify the annexation to Prussia of several million Poles, Slavs in race and language; nor a hundred and fifty thousand Danes in Schleswig who speak the Danish language. Moreover, even in regard to Alsace and Lorraine it is to be observed that the Germans were no slaves of their theory. In a considerable part of annexed Lorraine, French was the language spoken. Metz, the incomparable prize of the war, was as thoroughly French as Paris or Bordeaux. Even in annexed Alsace, there were considerable French speaking districts, in the southwest and in the valleys of the Vosges.

Manifestly the Germans are highly temperamental in their reasoning. A principle, which may be applied in the west, is not therefore necessarily to be applied in the east. Consistency, it has been affirmed, is but the hobgoblin of little minds.

Moreover, the rest of Europe would probably not relish the thorough application of the theory of language. Armed with it, Germany could go far; could annex a part of Belgium, that part which speaks Flemish, could annex Holland, two-thirds of Switzerland, and a good large block of Austria right down to the Adriatic. The present generation has surely no reason for regarding such a possibility as fantastic. This is the fundamental teaching of Pan-

Germanism whose power in modern Germany is sufficiently attested.

Apply the linguistic theory to Russia, apply it to Austria-Hungary and you will split those countries into probably twenty or more separate units. The theory is a double-edged sword, adapted to cut astonishing capers in the world.

But the Germans have still other arguments. In annexing Alsace-Lorraine, in drawing the western boundary as they did, they said that they were but establishing the "natural" boundary. In other words, the Vosges, being mountains, are a natural obstacle of importance, therefore a fit frontier, while the Rhine, being a river, is not one. Concerning this it may be said that the Vosges are not Alps, and that the Rhine has always been and will always be a formidable ditch to cross in the face of an enemy controlling the other side. Again, examining the actual line drawn in 1871, we note the same eclecticism on the part of the Germans. When it suited them they followed the crest of the Vosges; when it did not, they pushed their line farther west, with satisfaction to themselves but with conspicuous damage to their theory. Again the query naturally arises, as to what the Germans would prefer as a boundary, in case the French should be victorious in the present war. Would they prefer the river Rhine, or the mountains of the Black Forest, which are as high as the Vosges and which are in singular symmetry with the Vosges, lying about as far east of the Rhine as the latter do west of it. It is known to be unpleasant to be hoist with one's own petard.

Another argument greatly stressed by the Germans as a justification of the annexation of 1871 is the teaching of history. ⸤They urged incessantly their "historical rights." Alsace and Lorraine had once been included within the spacious and tenuous boundaries of the Holy Roman Empire. The annexation of what Louis XIV had torn from the Germany of that day, with the collusion of German princes who were rewarded according to their desire, was merely "resuming" what was one's own. Alsace and Lorraine, it is perfectly true, had been German lands before they had become French. But as Renan pointed out in 1870 they had been Celtic before that, and before the Celts had been the aborigines, and apes before the aborigines. "With the philosophy of history, as taught in Germany, nothing is legitimate in the world save the right of the orang-outangs unjustly dispossessed by the perfidy of civilized men."

So had Holland, so had Switzerland been parts

of the Holy Empire, so had Vienna, so had Prague. Was that a reason for "resuming" them, now that a new empire was in existence which was not a continuance and heir of the old but was based upon the overthrow of the old with its Hapsburg dynasty which had ruled for six centuries in unquestioned right? The appetite grows by that on which it feeds and in our own day the Pan-Germanists have risen to these heights of ambition but in 1871 sufficient unto the day were the ambitions thereof. Those who have read the preceding chapter of this book are in a position to appraise the merits of the historical argument. The matter is not as simple as it appears in German exegesis.

Leaving the shifting sands of explanation of the great act of 1871, we can easily gain more solid ground. The Germans annexed Alsace and Lorraine because they wanted them. The German "will to power" was not born yesterday or the day before. It has been a force long operating in the minds beyond the Rhine. All through the nineteenth century we can see it gaining expression and rising to *crescendo* with the development of militaristic Prussia. And German volition in this matter has not at all recognized the right of Alsace and Lorraine to have an opposite volition.

Military reasons were the primary reasons for the annexation of Alsace-Lorraine. The boundary was determined largely by the military men. They wished Metz and they took it, because, as Moltke said, it was the equivalent of an army of a hundred thousand men. They took Alsace because it would be, as Bismarck said, an admirable *glacis*, a military zone behind which is a fortress, a technical expression, signifying much.

The Germans wished Alsace-Lorraine also for economic reasons, for their mines of coal and iron.) They began the process of acquiring such lands at the expense of France, in 1815, as we have seen. They carried it much farther in 1871. It is to the frontier of 1871 that Germany is indebted for much of her industrial strength to-day, the basis of her political power and of her vaulting ambition. In 1913, out of 28,607,000 tons of iron ore extracted from German soil, 21,135,000 came from the mines of annexed Lorraine. To the rapes of 1815 and 1871, Germany owes much, as she is very well aware. The French, having lost their mines, subsequently discovered others in the part of Lorraine left to them in 1871, in the valley of the Briey.

In 1913, owing to the expansion of her industries, Germany was obliged to import from abroad fourteen million tons of iron ore. This is almost the exact amount annually extracted from the mines of Bricy, which Germany intends to keep, if she can, as a result of her present adventure in her time-honored profession of war. The Germans, who pride themselves on being realists and not romanticists in politics knew what they were aiming at in 1870 as in 1914. Their history is of a piece.

The reader should not imagine that the war of 1870 and the Treaty of Frankfort were impromptu occurrences, suddenly improvised out of a favoring, unexpected situation. A long period of preparation lay behind those events, as a long period of preparation lay behind the outbreak of the present war. The precise moment chosen for the actual beginning of hostilities was in both cases left necessarily to the conjunction of circumstances. A happy turn in the complex international life of Europe would furnish the opportune moment, the signal for the premeditated assault. There was a fruitful period of preparation of the minds of the German people for the forcible annexation of Alsace-Lorraine long before they were called upon by their rulers to accomplish the deed.

We have seen how gravely the two provinces were threatened at the time of the overthrow of Napoleon. The poet Arndt was the flaming spokesman of the passion of revenge, the desire of aggrandizement, which were aroused, particularly in the Prussians, by the bitterness of the Napoleonic wars. In his famous pamphlet "*The Rhine, Germany's River, not Germany's Boundary*," Arndt demanded not only the territories which the French had occupied since the Revolution on both banks of that river, but also Alsace, and in addition the banks of the Moselle, the Meuse, and the Sarre. His pamphlet evoked a widespread and eager response and was never forgotten in the decades that followed.[1] It exerted a durable influence upon the mind of Germany. Other pamphleteers, poets, and journalists started up at this resounding signal, repeating the same demands and even amplifying them with every variation of emphasis and eloquence, some claiming not only Alsace and Lorraine, but Luxemburg, the Netherlands, Franche-Comté, the "entire heritage of the Hapsburg and the Burgundian," as Arndt expressed it. The ideas and phrases of these writers were taken up by princes and generals. The Grand Duke of Baden declared that he wanted Strasburg, the King of

[1] I have used in this section the evidence gathered by Delahache in his *La carte au liséré vert*, pp. 53-66.

Württemberg that he desired all of Alsace, Prussians that they wished Alsace and Lorraine. The Prussian chauvinism was most aggressively personified in Blücher, Marshal Forward.

But the year 1815 passed without the desired dismemberment of France. England, Austria, and Russia, far from sympathizing with these clamorous ambitions, and not wishing to restore Louis XVIII to a discredited and therefore insecure throne, made only the limited demands for a rectification of the frontier which have already been described. France lost little, at that time, although that little was valuable.

German hopes were thus deferred but they were not extinguished. Germans were indignant at the Treaties of Vienna, which cheated them of their intended prey, and they nourished consequently one grievance the more. Whenever in subsequent years the European sky grew dark, the same thunders were heard rumbling round the horizon. Every international crisis aroused the combative spirit and sharpened the acquisitive instinct. Arndt continued his fiery appeals and Becker wrote his "German Rhine," which echoed throughout the land. The future emperor William I, then Prince of Prussia, also tried his hand at poetry not thereby greatly enriching the German anthology, as his Pegasus possessed only a limited afflatus, but nevertheless reënforcing from his lofty coign of vantage the general temper of the times.

> "The Rhine must become
> Throughout its entire course
> The possession of the German lands!
> Fling out your banner!
> And you, O people of the Vosges
> And of the forests of Ardennes
> We wish to deliver you
> From the yoke of the alien impostor
> . . . .
> So that some day your children
> May be Germans
> And may honor the conquerors,
> Of their fathers!"

In 1841 Moltke, the Marshal that was to be, expounded in a German review the theory of German rights to Alsace and Lorraine, interlarding his exposition with unrestrained threats to France. She should know the power of the German Sword!

Year after year it was the same refrain, not uttered discreetly and in hushed tones but with full-throated power, by journalists, professors, students. Any dissonant note was drowned in instant disapproval as for instance when a publicist, named Charles Biedermann, dared to ask if anyone seriously believed that Alsace would voluntarily renounce France "which assured her everything that thoughtful people elsewhere wished to secure for themselves."

In 1846, the King of Würtemberg said to Bismarck: "We must have Strasburg. The heart of the matter is Strasburg. As long as she is not German, the states of South Germany will not be able to share in the political life of Germany."

The meetings of learned societies, the relations of student bodies were embittered by this ever-present preoccupation. In 1861, Kirschleger, a well-known botanist and professor at the University of Strasburg, attending a congress of naturalists at Speyer and being told by his fellow scientists that Alsace must be returned to the confederation replied: "You ought at least to ask if we have any desire to return to you. . . . We wish to remain Frenchmen."

In 1867, when the Luxemburg affair aroused France and Germany to a dangerous pitch of feeling, the students of the University of Strasburg sent an address to the students of Germany, a part of which ran as follows:

"War we do not wish, national hatreds we do not feel. Without doubt, if war were inevitable, we would not hesitate over the sacrifices we would make for France, but, now, while there is still time we come to offer you our hand and to ask your coöperation in defending in both our countries, the cause of peace and liberty. . . . Unite Germany, but for freedom and progress, and we too will fulfil our task in the same spirit."

To this dignified appeal came a freezing blast from the students of Berlin:

"Renegades and turncoats are detested by all men everywhere, and you will form no exception. . . . At a time when the small nations, the Greeks, the Roumanians, the Serbs, the Slavs are awakening from their torpor, and are recalling their nationalities, you, Alsatians and Lorrainers, you should not remain apathetic. What! you would be willing to renounce your nationality! . . . to march against Germany, our mother and yours! What! you would be willing to stab your Alma Mater in the bosom? Quit being bastards, students of Alsace and Lorraine, become again in your hearts real children of the German fatherland. Then we too, when we shall have conquered in the next war, as conquer we shall without doubt, will press you in fraternal embrace to our breasts. But before then, never! *Dixmus et salvavimus animam.*"

This stern rebuke of the students of Berlin was

not the last word in tact but has its obvious importance as an historical document.

Thus the official world, the army, the press, and the school were all coöperating in laying the bases of the future, and in urging the remaking of the map of Europe. There were Pan-Germanists in abundance long before the present. The war of 1914 was not the only one long and steadily prepared by the leaders of the German people, each in his several way. Even the ninety-three professors who instructed an obscurantist world so authoritatively in 1914 were but reënacting an ancient *geste*. When in 1870 the war broke out between Germany and France the celebrities of the universities stood embattled, in serried ranks, headed by Theodore Mommsen, the leader of them all, who published in certain Italian newspapers his letters, "To the People of Italy," in which he announced the intention of Germany to annex Alsace and Lorraine. Others intoned the self-same chant, among whom the most conspicuous were William Maurenbrecher, Professor of History in the University of Königsberg and Adolph Wagner, Professor of Economics in the University of Leipsic. Wagner, in his pamphlet said, among many other things, that Germany must have Alsace and "German Lorraine" with Metz, although Metz was "two miles beyond the linguistic frontier." Then after the victory a solid military establishment must be set up there. "We will not permit the neutralization of Alsace and Lorraine! We have already had quite enough neutralizations, to our injury. Alsace and Lorraine must be incorporated in a healthy and vigorous state, in Germany, in Prussia, marching at the head of Imperial Germany." And Professor Wagner closed by announcing that "God wills it! (*Das walte Gott!*)"

What a plagiarist the Germany of our day is may be seen by anyone who cares to dip into this prebellum literature of the Bismarckian era. The same hatreds then as now, the same assertions of superiority, the same intimate revelations of the wishes of the Deity; poets, historians, philosophers, editors, politicians, vying in noble emulation for the hegemony in this campaign of slander and contempt tinged, it might be pointed out, with envy and with fear.

What did they fear? The answer may be briefly given. They feared the French Revolution, the principles of '89, principles which sounded the doom of feudalism, of absolute monarchy, so ardently admired in Germany. The revolutionary nation must be put down with its pernicious principles which carry a deadly blight wherever they go and undermine the sacred Ark of the Covenant, the loyalty to monarchs. Such was the prevailing note in the polemics of pre-bellum Germany. As shaped and directed by Bismarck the political evolution of Germany was intended to be, and was, a chapter in the Counter-Revolution which has been in the process of execution in Europe ever since 1789 and which is now, perhaps, approaching its final pages.

One more aspect of this verbal and literary campaign against France, which preceded the military campaign, and the picture is complete. The famous immorality of the French must be denounced, and it was, with zest. A typical remark was that of General Scharnhorst, whose profession in many countries is synonymous with honoring your possible enemy, a remark made in 1840 and to the effect that "France represents the principle of immorality" and that if she is not annihilated, then there is "no longer a God in Heaven." Scharnhorst was only a general but when his ethical and theological dicta were confirmed by those who were specialists in these high matters, they appeared to have all the finality that could be expected or desired. The finishing strokes to this indictment of

France which preceded and accompanied the war of 1870 were furnished by the clergy. A single example is sufficient. Pastor Schroeder, Doctor of Theology and Court Preacher in Berlin, declared that the French were "a people gravely stricken with the leprosy of sin," that it had "lost all sense of its better self" because of its lack of "discipline, its immodesty, and impiety."

It only remained to be said that "God was now to inflict upon this people the trial by blood and iron" and that this war was "the judgment of God." Consequently, these things were said, by respected and confident ministers of the gospel, by the ghostly monitors of a people whose piety and morality were supposedly above reproach, thoroughly attested as they were by themselves.

Such was the background of German national thought and feeling, against which the annexation of Alsace and Lorraine can only properly be envisaged.

CHAPTER IV

THE VICTIM'S PRIVILEGE

By Article I of the Treaty of Frankfort, Alsace and Lorraine were ceded to the German Empire. That the people of the ceded provinces had any rights whatever in the matter was not for a moment admitted by the German government. Their consent was not requisite to the validity of the transaction. The idea of allowing them to vote on the subject of separation was dismissed summarily, as soon as suggested. The principle of the plebiscite has never won the esteem of Prussian statesmen. Appeal to it has always been sedulously avoided in the case of Prussian annexations.

By Article II of the treaty, the people of Alsace-Lorraine acquired their one privilege. They were to have until October 1, 1872, to decide, individually, whether they would preserve their French citizenship or become German subjects. If they should choose the former they must by that date have actually withdrawn from Alsace or Lorraine and have physically established themselves in France. This was their option. It was made clear that no one could opt for France and at the same time remain in Alsace-Lorraine. As the fatal day approached, and indeed all through the spring and summer of 1872, the agitation of the people increased, as they confronted the bitter choice. Many postponed the decision until the final moment and the trains going westward were, during the last few days, crowded with those who had decided to expatriate themselves rather than don the livery of subjection to the hated foreigner. Pathetic and heartbreaking were the signs of distress and sorrow that accompanied this hegira, unprecedented in the enlightened and humane nineteenth century and in the heart of Europe, of a people attached by all the ties of affection and interest to their native and ancestral fields and villages. The public opinion of Europe was profoundly moved by these harrowing scenes.

Consider this problem from the point of view of the Alsatians and Lorrainers. Option for France meant emigration, meant leaving behind all that was dear, all that made life sweet or tolerable. A more poignant dilemma it would be hard to imagine. What was their duty under the conditions in which they found themselves, what ought to be their line of conduct, both for their own interest and the interest of the country from which they were now torn. The problem would have been bewildering and distressing had they had to do with a tactful and considerate conqueror. Instead they faced a conqueror not known for any sympathetic instincts nor for any excessive magnanimity toward the defeated and the powerless, a conqueror hard, determined, exultant, and intoxicated with success.

An agonizing choice which one needs little imagination to picture, an individual decision relentlessly imposed upon every member of the community. To quit the land of one's nativity, to leave the place where one belongs and where one's ancestors have lived from generation to generation, to leave one's profession, or trade, or craft or farm, to break up one's career and launch forth upon an unknown sea, to begin life again and under new surroundings, and with formidable risks at best, these are the concrete and painful consequences of a change in the boundaries of nations, of which we speak so lightly, without vividly appreciating the suffering, the confusion, the dismay they may impose. The intimate and intricate personal problem came home in all severity and peremptoriness to every individual in Alsace-Lorraine in 1872.[1]

[1] The subject has been admirably presented in a monograph by Georges Delahache, *L'Exode*. Also, by the same author, in *La carte au liséré vert*, pp. 95–125.

One of the conspicuous classes immediately affected was that of the magistrates of the courts. Rich rewards were in store for any judge who would coöperate with the new régime. For the "conversion" of a person of such dignity and reputation would be regarded as a brilliant stroke by the conqueror, worthy of exceptional favors. Whereas if the judge were to opt for France, how could he find the equivalent of what he would lose? All judicial positions in France were filled already by those who needed them now more than ever. And there would be fewer positions than before owing to the decrease of territory. On the other hand, if they remained, these former French judges would be obliged to interpret and decide in such a way as to strengthen and consolidate the new system, to enforce and sanction all the police measures the conqueror might decree, to speak the language of the victor. To this rôle of remunerated servility the judges of Alsace-Lorraine could not bring themselves to submit. All but six of them left for France.

Judges were few but school teachers were numerous. If they remained they were assured larger salaries than they had ever received. If they rejected the favoring winds of fortune what positions could they hope to find? On the other hand, if they remained the iron would enter into their souls every day anew. They would have to teach history as the Germans taught it, with an aggressive patriotism to which all impartiality and all fairness were alien. They would have to instruct the youth of their provinces that German rule was an unalloyed good; that Charlemagne was a German Emperor and nothing but a German; that Alsace had been insidiously ravished by Louis XIII and Louis XIV; that Frederick II, however, was a great king for having taken Silesia and Poland; that Germany really included Denmark, part of Belgium, part of Holland, part of Switzerland, not a little of what was left of France. And above all they would be obliged to teach that the annexation by the Germans of Alsace-Lorraine was not a conquest but a legitimate recovery of stolen property. In such an intellectual atmosphere it would be difficult to breathe. Many felt the shame of it, and opted for France.

At the end of 1872 only 20 per cent of all the officials of Alsace-Lorraine were natives of those provinces.

One could run through every class of society from the highest officials to the humblest peasant and workingman and show in detail how a diplomatic document may react disastrously upon every individual in his attempt to earn a livelihood. Every human soul had its crisis to confront and to surmount. A general overthrow, for a while, perhaps for long, of the personal existence of every individual, self-interest wrestling with sentiment, emotion with hard necessity.

There was added the tangled question of where duty lay. Would not one show a greater loyalty in remaining in Alsace than in leaving? To leave was to abandon the field to Germanizing immigrants, to remain was to contest every step in the threatened process of Germanization. Which protest would be more effective, to quit the country or to stay and fight it out, trying to preserve the local patrimony, the ancestral heritage of institutions and traditions, against overwhelming odds? Duty was not clear. Either choice was compounded of bitterness and suffering. Beside the fears or chances of the future, in every home arose the question, and rapidly became predominant, should the sons become German soldiers as they would be required to become if they remained in Alsace-Lorraine? Then again why desert the country, why not stay and fight for it, in stubborn, passive, resolute ways, against the coming German invasion?

By the first of October, 1872, nearly 60,000 persons had departed. Many never saw again the ancestral roof. Many, thus ruthlessly uprooted from all that men hold most dear paid the ransom of their country in sadness and in long-continued misery, until death came to end the cruel agony. One hundred and sixty thousand had opted for France but of these the German government annulled 100,000 on the ground that the options had not been accompanied with actual removal. Now and then an entire town or village withdrew. Bischwiller, a town of 11,500 inhabitants, saw nearly half its population transport itself *en masse* to Elbeuf in Normandy. The exodus of Alsatians continued year after year, from seven to twelve thousand on an average leaving annually for France. ' From 1905 to 1910 even, an examination of official statistics shows that 50,000 Alsatians emigrated from their country. M. Eccard says that the fact of annexation and the subsequent dislike of the German régime caused more than half a million Alsatians and Lorrainers to leave their homes, and these generally were among the most independent and energetic inhabitants. "What the emigration has cost us in population amounts to hundreds of thousands; in money to billions; in capacity and intelligence, no estimate can be made. The loss is irreparable.[1]"

The Germans had proclaimed themselves the "liberators" of their long lost brothers. They had asseverated in every accent and with every emphasis that the children snatched from them by iniquitous Louis XIV were eagerly awaiting the end of their captivity and that great would be their joy when once more they found themselves around the family hearth. To be sure no cry had ever gone up from the Alsatians for deliverance. And now came the passionate and unanimous protests, those submitted by the Alsatians and Lorrainers at Bordeaux in 1871 and later in Berlin in 1874. In the presence of such an attitude and in the face of this continuous emigration, born of desperation, it was not possible long to continue the refrain about the release of the much suffering brothers. The Germans, therefore, angry and humiliated at the spectacle, adopted another shibboleth, more appropriate to the situation. "We know better how to govern Alsace than the Alsatians know themselves," said Treitschke, thus giving the new note which was

[1] The movement continued for many years, has, indeed, been uninterrupted since 1871. From 1875-1880 about 35,000 emigrated; from 1880-1885 about 60,000, from 1885-1890 about 37,000; from 1890-1895 about 34,000.

to prevail from that day to this in the conduct of the Empire toward the unhappy provinces. If the Alsatians refused to see a benefactor in the German Empire nevertheless the benefaction should take place. Benefactions can be imposed, even if not joyously welcomed by the selected recipient. The heavy hand, as well as the light touch, can mould the human clay. Men are plastic and can be made by Prussians into the likeness of Prussians. It may take time and the process may be characterized by annoying friction. But time is to be had cheaply by biding it, and the transformation will proceed without haste, without rest. In determining to incorporate the Alsatians by force into the German family and mould them without asking or awaiting their consent Germany was but using a policy which Prussia had often employed. In the presence of the past achievements of "blood and iron" no sane person could deny their efficacy. The Germans had appeared in Alsace proclaiming with their customary naïveté the superiority of their "culture" and convinced that it would be immediately recognized. But they soon found their error, and were mortified and indignant. The "conquest" of Alsace must evidently be made without the coöperation of the Alsatians. It would manifestly be a longer task than had been anticipated.

Prussia had been made by force and Prussia had made the German Empire by force. In 1866 Hanover, Schleswig-Holstein, Hesse-Cassel, Nassau and Frankfort had been annexed forthwith by right of military conquest. No plebiscites had been held, as in Italy at the time of her unification, and as in Savoy and Nice at the time of their annexation to France. "We must make Italy by liberty, or we must give up trying to make her," Cavour, the architect and builder of Italian unity, had said and had made his deeds conform to his words. Such methods, involving the right of the people to determine their own destinies, were despised and scorned by Bismarck and they played no part whatever in the making of the present German Empire. Force can accomplish miracles in the future as it has accomplished in the past. Its miraculous qualities were now to be tested in Alsace and Lorraine and would no doubt be equally apparent. There would be manifest advantage too in stamping out in another region of the world the pestilential heresy, born of the impious French Revolution, about the right of the governed. Two centuries of French domination had naturally made the Alsatians degenerates. Their ideas must be set right again, their morale raised by severe discipline. As masters in the art of severe discipline, that is, in the art of subjecting the wills of millions of men to those of a small self-constituted minority, the Germans had every right to plume themselves. This was and is, and their rulers intend, ever shall be their message to the world.

Discipline was therefore now applied to these degenerates who loved the freedom of France more than the bondage of Prussia. But bondage is the best school of discipline.

CHAPTER V

ALSACE-LORRAINE, 1871-1890

ALTHOUGH the annexation of Alsace-Lorraine was regarded by the Germans, not as a conquest, but as a "recovery" of what was theirs, nevertheless these provinces were treated and have been treated, ever since 1871, as conquered territory and in the approved and standardized Prussian fashion. Arbitrary and dictatorial government, sometimes partially disguised but generally open and harsh, has held the victims of the Treaty of Frankfort as in a vise. Asserting with vocal unanimity and with wearisome iteration that the Alsatians were Germans through and through, the government with doubtful consistency adopted at the outset and has steadily followed a policy of Germanization, thus confessing the falsity of its assumption. A sufficient comment on the success of this policy was furnished in 1914 when a high official of the Empire declared that Alsace was "the enemy's country."

The methods used in this process were in no sense original. They were the traditional ones long in use in unhappy Europe for the dragooning of recalcitrant peoples. Metternich knew them in his day, and Frederick the Great in his. The Prussian mind, the most conservative in Europe, tenacious not open, kept steadily and heavily along in the familiar groove. No dallying with hazardous experiments in winning the unwilling such as England had indulged in, to her great advantage, in Canada and elsewhere. For German statesmen every question is a Machtfrage or question of might. As to the efficacy of sheer "power" the history of Alsace-Lorraine since 1871 has something to say. The Germans have certainly never discovered the song the sirens sang. Legislation and administration, barracks and schools, money and menaces, these are the time-honored weapons of attack to which any people, no matter how wilful or stiff-necked, must in the end succumb. An attentive and ubiquitous police is a useful monitor to the wayward.

The political organization devised by Germany for her conquered territories was based upon the principle that they were to be ruled without their consent. It was at first proposed that they should be divided up among Prussia, Bavaria, and Baden, their neighbors, a partition in the Polish fashion. But this would have aroused the jealousy of the other German states which had shared in the conquest and wished also to share in the booty. Another proposal was that they should be incorporated in Prussia alone, the sole German state, it was held, capable of digesting so important a prey. For some time the matter was in suspense until finally the idea was adopted that they should constitute an Imperial Territory, a *Reichsland*, which would belong in common to the twenty-five states which composed the German Empire. But the Reichsland should not be a state, like each of the other twenty-five, sovereign within its sphere, self-governing, but it should be governed, in the name of the Empire, by its head, the King of Prussia. There would be obvious advantages in such an arrangement, advantages pointed out by Bismarck in a speech of May 25, 1871. The jealousy of the various states of Germany would not be aroused; it would be easy with such a form of government to avoid granting any political rights whatever to the Alsatians and Lorrainers which would not be possible were they incorporated outright in the neighboring states, the subjects of which possessed certain rights. Moreover this device would make all the members of the confederation, big and little, accomplices in the dismemberment of France, and, consequently guardians of the conquests. The cohesive power of public plunder is well known. And, moreover, William I would really be the undisputed master of the Reichsland, not as King of Prussia, it is true, but as German Emperor, which would do as well and would be, for all practical purposes, quite the same thing.

This point settled, the Reichsland was divided into three "presidencies," Upper Alsace, Lower Alsace, and Lorraine and these in turn into "circles," of which Upper Alsace was to have six, Lower Alsace eight, Lorraine eight, each circle to be administered by a Director.

Over the Reichsland as a whole stood a President-Superior who was subject to the supervision of the Alsace-Lorraine Division of the Chancery in Berlin. But the Chancellor, who was responsible only to the Emperor, might at any moment change his attitude or policy toward a people which were entirely unrepresented either in the local government or in the Reichstag or in the Bundesrath.

Such was the initial form of government vouchsafed by the conqueror to a people of whom Treitschke in a lyrical outburst had prophesied that the day would come when in the remotest village of the Vosges the Alsatian peasant would exclaim, "O the joy and happiness of being a citizen of the Empire."

Treitschke was not keenly sensitive to the difference between being a citizen and an abject subject, bereft of rights. Servitude of a people who had long been fundamentally democratic could go no farther. In the sixteenth century, under Hapsburg rule, the Alsatians were far freer and more independent than they were at the close of the nineteenth century under the Hohenzollerns. Yet it is one of the boasts of Germans that the present empire is the authentic continuance of the old Holy Roman Empire whose sway was at any rate far more benign, however inefficient it may have been. The Alsatians have been ever since 1871 slaves of another's will.

The position of the provinces has been peculiar, exceptional. The German Empire is a confederation of independent, self-governing states. But of these states Alsace-Lorraine is not one. She is a sort of undivided property held in common for the other twenty-five and primarily for their advantage. She was not to be the mistress of her own political life. The laws which were to govern her were to be framed by the Bundesrath, an assembly of delegates appointed by the rulers of the twenty-five states and a body in which she was entirely unrepresented. Moreover, over such laws the Emperor was to have an absolute veto. Every one of the twenty-five possessed autonomy, and was in a position to preserve and accentuate her own personality by individual legislation on matters which came home to her citizens in the course of every day, education, relations of church and state, industry. The individuality, the distinctive needs or wishes of each component state, thus had a wide sphere for self-expression and could secure therefore a large measure of contentment for its citizens, could preserve their self-respect. Not so with Alsace-Lorraine. No sphere of independent legislation was open to her. The Bundesrath and the Emperor held her in absolute tutelage. She was a subject, a subject of the Empire as a whole.

Over her hung like a pall the law of December 30, 1871, whose Article 10, the famous Dictatorship Article, established and legalized arbitrary government in its simplest form. "In the case of danger for the public safety, the President-Superior is authorized to take all measures which he may consider necessary to prevent this danger. He is, in particular, authorized to exercise, in the district threatened, the powers conferred upon the military authorities in the case of the state of siege by the law of August 9, 1849." He has the right, in order to execute these measures, to call out all the troops stationed in Alsace-Lorraine. Article 9 of the law of August 9, 1849, ran as follows: "The military authority has the right to search by day or by night the domiciles of the citizen; to remove old offenders and the individuals whose domiciles are not in the places subjected to the state of siege; to order the surrender of arms and munitions, and to search for them and to seize them; to forbid all publications and meetings which he considers calculated to excite or encourage disorder."

Thus the chief executive of the Reichsland had the right to grant himself the power whenever he wished to, and without limitation of time or place, to take "all measures" he might judge necessary, including the right to expel citizens from the country, even if they were not charged with any crime, and even when domiciled outside the region subject to the state of siege.

This law remained in force until June 9, 1902. At any moment it could be invoked to make waste paper of whatever apparent privileges might be granted in the course of the years to the people of the conquered land. The representative of the

Emperor in Alsace might at any moment suppress any individual whom he judged annoying. As long as that article remained in force, arbitrary, despotic government was the fundamental law of the land, the system that might be in abeyance for long periods of time, but that might be put into force at any instant. A Damocles sword hung over every Alsatian head. This was the dominant feature in the life of the Reichsland, which must never be lost sight of, in spite of the fact that, during any given period, its actual exercise might be suspended.

Changes of detail in the system of government of Alsace-Lorraine have been made at various times since 1871. They have not altered the fundamental fact that the Alsatians are an entirely subject people with no rights whatever which they can call their own; with no privileges which cannot at any moment be withdrawn or modified by a power outside themselves.

On January 1, 1874, the constitution of the German Empire was introduced into Alsace-Lorraine. This brought two changes in the organization of the country. Henceforth, laws specially applicable to it instead of being promulgated by the Emperor, with the consent of the Bundesrath alone, must also have the consent of the Reichstag. And henceforth Alsace-Lorraine would have the right to send fifteen representatives to the Reichstag, as if she were a state of the Empire. She was to have, unlike the states of the Empire, no representatives in the Bundesrath, far and away the most important political body in the Empire. The first fifteen representatives chosen in conformity with this arrangement renewed in forceful language the protest of Bordeaux, as we have seen. In 1874, was instituted also the Delegation or Landesauschuss, a sort of local legislature, or rather a simulacrum of a legislature since it was, in fact, simply a consultative committee which might or might not be asked its opinion of legislation under consideration by the authorities in Berlin and destined for the Reichsland.

More important were the laws of 1879, enacting the so-called Constitution of Alsace-Lorraine (July 4). The President-Superior, whose function had been to transmit business affecting the Reichsland, now gave way to a Statthalter, or lieutenant-governor, appointed by the Emperor and exercising the powers previously vested in the Chancellor. The Landesauschuss was nearly doubled in size. This was the form of government which existed in Alsace-Lorraine during the next thirty-two years, from 1879 to 1911. The executive power was vested in the Emperor who was to appoint, dismiss, and act through the Statthalter, who, in turn, was assisted by a Secretary of State and by four heads of departments (Interior and Education; Justice and Public Worship; Finance; Commerce, Agriculture and Public Works). The executive was not responsible to the legislature, but was responsible to the Emperor alone. The Landesauschuss was, henceforth, to consist of fifty-eight members. It was also given the right to propose laws, to initiate legislation. But no more than before was it to be an independent local parliament, enacting local legislation, like the diets of Bavaria, Baden, and Würtemberg. No bills could become law without the consent of the Bundesrath, that is the princes of Germany, in which body Alsace-Lorraine was to have no vote.

By this Constitution of 1879 the government made concessions to the party which demanded self-government for Alsace-Lorraine; but it did not concede self-government. The Statthalter, it should never be forgotten, could exercise at any moment the power given him by the so-called Dictatorship Article. He was responsible to the Emperor alone. Legislation was henceforth normally to be enacted by the Bundesrath and the Landesauschuss. But it might, however, at any moment be made by the Bundesrath and the Reichstag who might disregard entirely the local legislature (the Landesauschuss) and local opinion. It might justly be said of the so-called constitutional history of Alsace-Lorraine that the more it changed the more it was the same thing.

Such was the form of government elaborated for Alsace-Lorraine during the first decade of German rule. The constitution of 1879 was destined to remain unaltered for over thirty years. The government offered the Alsatians no guarantees whatever of life, liberty or the pursuit of happiness. As a concession to the spirit of autonomy it was derisory. The despotism of the authorities of Berlin was not even decently veiled but was frank and unabashed. Its essential spirit was expressed by General von Werder when he said: "I hate the Alsatians because they love France." Hertzog, a high official, admitted publicly in 1872 that "the idealism deeply rooted in the soul of the German people had not been able to make its way into the heart of the Alsatians," but asserted that, nevertheless, its victory was assured. Bismarck, who in the early days of the annexation had professed a lively and sympathetic and probably insincere interest in the Alsatians, irritated by the progress of events, blurted out his real feeling in a speech on November 30, 1874, saying that Alsace had not been annexed because of her *beaux yeux*, but simply and solely because she would furnish an excellent military defense of the Empire, an important first line fortification, and that Germany was equally indifferent to Alsatian lamentations and Alsatian wrath. This typically brutal and contemptuous outburst of high Prussian tact and "statesmanship" was, of course, profoundly resented by all Alsatians and Lorrainers, and has never been forgotten. It needed no specialist in psychology to point out that this was not the best way to gain an entrance into the hearts of the people. But such were then and are still considered in Prussia the surest methods of solidly establishing the state. Other Bismarckian gloss on the difficult art of statecraft had already been furnished by the Iron Chancellor in the session of May 16, 1873, when in reply to an attack by Windhorst, leader of the Center Party, upon the dictatorial policy being followed by the government in Alsace-Lorraine, he scornfully exclaimed: "We Prussians and North Germans are not famous for knowing how to make friends gracefully and for handling disagreeable questions with courtesy."

The actual measures adopted and enforced in the Imperial Territory were in harmony with the spirit of these utterances. The articles of the Treaty of Frankfort were interpreted and executed in the narrowest and severest sense. The actual determination of the new boundaries, mile by mile, by the engineers appointed for the purpose, was characterized by much sharp practice and by incessant bullying. The enforcement of the people's right of option was literal and technical to a degree. The recruiting of young Alsatians into the Prussian army, the most agonizing and galling feature of this new situation for the Alsatians whose fathers had just been fighting desperately for France, was begun at the earliest possible moment and rigidly carried out in 1872. Obligatory military service in what the Alsatians could only regard as the enemy's army was a hateful thing, rendered all the more odious by the certain knowledge that the recruits would be sent far from home for their training, to the provinces of Old Prussia. Very numerous were those who sought escape from the ignominy by flight. Thousands of young men took the road to France, leaving their families, perhaps forever, and running the risk of loss of property rather than submit.

The army and the schools were intended by the

authorities to be the chief agencies in the policy of Germanization on which the government was bent from the start. Even before Alsace and Lorraine were theirs by treaty the administration had begun to wield the weapon of education. Its first act was to eliminate almost completely the study of French from the curriculum of the schools, at the same time ordaining universal and obligatory attendance and increasing the salaries of the teachers. When the study of French was not entirely suppressed it was relegated to a peculiar place. The curriculum of the school in Mulhouse, as described by a speaker in the Reichstag in 1872, prescribed the teaching "of history in German, of geography in German, of penmanship in French (laughter) of drawing in French (laughter)."

In addition to all this, the police everywhere furnished an additional irritant to the public mind by their petty inquisition and general meddlesomeness. Important members of the community were expelled by summary process. The mayor of Strasburg was removed from his office, the city council, protesting against this infringement of its rights as it chose the mayor, was rewarded by dissolution, and from 1873 to 1886 Strasburg was at the mercy of one man, Back, appointed acting mayor by the Emperor and exercising all the powers of both mayor and city council.

Thus was autocratic government of the purest type rapidly installed in a country which had never known it, which for centuries under the Holy Roman Empire had enjoyed in its "Ten Free Cities," its republics of Strasburg and Mulhouse, free and antonomous political institutions, a country which had joined joyously in the French Revolution because the new French democracy was naturally congenial to the traditional democratic sentiments of the Alsatians. As an Alsatian writer has expressed it, "France became what we had been; and what we wished to be we became through her." "The Alsatian," says Lichtenberger, "is temperamentally republican. He has never been subject to the authority of a national dynasty. . . . What made the French army so popular with the Alsatians was its democratic origin."

Now, however, the Alsatians were subjected to a national dynasty with a vengeance, and they seized the first opportunity they had to express their opinion of their fate. In view of all the circumstances which have been passed in review it is no occasion for surprise that the initial act of the first representatives ever sent to the Reichstag was the protest of 1874, whose echoes have not yet died away, whose phrases have an almost uncanny actuality and applicability to the present moment.

Gradually during the next five years the political organization of the annexed provinces was worked out, as already indicated, on the basis of the complete and absolute supremacy of the Empire, and the so-called Constitution of 1879 was the result. Henceforth the Alsatians were to have an assembly, called the Delegation, or Landesauschuss, whose opinion on measures concerning Alsace-Lorraine might be asked, if it pleased the authorities to ask it. At least henceforth there would be a representative of the Emperor resident in Strasburg, and in a position to understand the wishes and needs of the people and to act as a sympathetic and intelligent mediator between the authorities in Berlin and their Alsatian subjects. There was an opportunity here for a useful rôle of moderation and conciliation.

The first Statthalter, under the new régime, Field Marshal von Manteuffel, attempted to carry on the government in just this spirit, not abating in the slightest degree the pretensions to unlimited power and to exact obedience asserted by his government, but seeking to seduce the Alsatians by tactful conduct and by the blandishments of courtesy and sympathy. His was a policy, if need be, of the iron hand encased in a velvet glove.

Manteuffel had had a long and important career. The appointment of a man of his distinction as first Statthalter was supposed to express a subtle flattery to the people whom he came to rule from the imperial palace in Strasburg. Manteuffel had filled many offices, military and diplomatic, had commanded the fifteenth army corps in the Franco-German war, and the Army of Occupation in France after that war was over, in the discharge of which function he had had an opportunity to display all his attractive and ingratiating qualities of mind and manner, his understanding, his moderation, his tact. He had gained the respect of the French under conditions which were unfavorable and exacting. He now made his solemn entry into Strasburg on October 1, 1879, and entered upon a task for which his long experience, his diplomatic dexterity, his conciliatory and kindly nature seemed preëminently to fit him. He was seventy years of age, was somewhat broken by his long and arduous services to the state, and would have preferred a life of repose; but at the personal request of Emperor William I, in whose confidence he was, he undertook the new duty, sincerely anxious to make his mission beneficent and honorable. But he was destined to learn that however blessed are the peacemakers in this world, their work is frequently but vanity and vexation of spirit.

The first and not the least of his vexations came from his own official family, from the administrators of various grades whose characters illustrated the stiffness and the arrogance of the Prussian bureaucracy rather than the conciliatory graces, and who worked behind his back against the policy he adopted, seeking surreptitiously and venomously to discredit him in the high quarters of Berlin. The leader of these was Hertzog, the chief minister, a man who had been up to that time the head of the Alsace-Lorraine section of the Chancellery, a typically rigid and peremptory Prussian official, who quite naturally thought the system he had hitherto presided over and shaped in Berlin entirely satisfactory, and needing no change; whose personal manners, too, were offensive to the Alsatians.

The "Manteuffel Era," as this period of Alsatian history is called, lasted six years, from 1879 to 1885. If anyone could have succeeded in the rôle he had mapped out Manteuffel could have. Believing correctly that no government is successful for any lengt' of time that does not have the people on its side, M' teuffel sought first to know those among whom he had come to rule. He travelled much through the country, trying to impart his ideas to local officials and notabilities, municipal councilors, clergymen, and teachers, to say the happy and healing word to everyone. He told the people of Alsace and Lorraine that he understood and respected their sentiments, that he did not ask for an enthusiastic adhesion to the new order of things, but only a reasoned submission to the ineluctable fact. He warned them, however, that he would proceed *à outrance* against anyone who should conspire with the foreigner. He announced that as the Doge of Venice had solemnly wedded the Adriatic, so he wished to woo Alsace-Lorraine and obtain her liberties for her. For six years Manteuffel tried but tried in vain to win the assent, the affection implied in his reference to the Doge. In his personal capacity he won general esteem. Accessible to all, receiving freely even workingmen who came to present their grievances, he exemplified the fine politeness of the Old Régime, speaking and writing French on unofficial occasions, greeting acquaintances first when he met them in his solitary walks about Strasburg, helping some old woman whose vegetable cart had gotten stuck in the mud to get it out, he was a more popular figure than his predecessor or than any of his successors were to be.

But there was a fundamental incompatibility of temper between the wooer and the wooed which no amount of kindliness and tact could dissipate. "I am bound to respect the sentiments which lie in the nature of things after this country has lived for two centuries in communion with France," Manteuffel said to the Delegation in 1880. But the trouble was this very nature of things. The Alsatians, grateful for the greater mildness shown them, for the freer atmosphere they were breathing, nevertheless instinctively and instantly withdrew within themselves whenever asked to give any evidence of German sentiments. If there was an ineluctable fact, there was also an ineluctable difficulty, a gulf which no bridge could span.

In his fundamental purpose Manteuffel could not succeed. Moreover, he did not have the support of his own officials whose conduct served more or less to nullify and insulate the Statthalter. All through his regency the bureaucrats of Alsace-Lorraine, big and little, carried on an incessant and perfidious campaign in the German press, seeking to undermine him. Harassed by the Germans who criticised his moderation and irritated by the Alsatians and Lorrainers whose passive resistance to the one thing that counted revealed the essential superficiality of the "pacification," moreover compelled from time to time in the discharge of his obligations to the authorities in Berlin to adopt harsh and unpopular measures, such as the suppression of certain newspapers, thus showing, as by lightning strokes the essential fragility of their "liberties," Manteuffel stood insecurely upon treacherous sands. So strong was the opposition to his policy in Germany that he would have been recalled had it not been that the octogenarian Emperor, William I, did not like to dismiss old friends and advisers. Nevertheless, in the long run William I was accustomed to do, not what he liked himself, but what Bismarck liked, and Bismarck was known to be commenting on Manteuffel's blunders and lack of success. The lack of success was, however, not due to Manteuffel but to Bismarck, whose policy of annexation had made it inevitable. How complete that lack was, was strikingly shown in the elections to the Reichstag in 1881 and 1884. Alsace and Lorraine elected, as in 1874, fifteen "protesters," despite severe official pressure.

Manteuffel's programme, the only wise one, could only succeed if assured of length of years for its realization. And these were not to be vouchsafed the sagacious experiment. The Germans have never shown any faith in benignant processes, in trusting to patience and the lapse of time to accomplish the work of Germanization. Manteuffel's official days were numbered. But he was spared the crowning humiliation of recall because his earthly days were also numbered. He died on June 17, 1885, and the policy for which he stood died with him. His era remains the only attractive one, with all its defects, in the history of German rule in Alsace-Lorraine. The administration which was to follow it was to be of an entirely different tone and character, was to be pitched in a different and a very strident key.

As the Manteuffel régime had not, in the brief space of six years, reconciled Alsace to Germany, as the process of comparatively mild Germanization had made no appreciable advance, the German government now resorted to methods with which it was more familiar, and in which it had a more robust faith. Coercion, pure and simple, coercion thorough and undisguised, applied at every point considered dangerous and applied without hesitation and without interruption, was henceforth the programme of the government. To preside over the execution of this policy a new Statthalter, Prince Chlodwig von Hohenlohe-Schillingsfürst was appointed. A member of the royal family, an uncle of the Empress, a former ambassador in Paris, as cold and reserved as Manteuffel had been cordial and even expansive, a lean man with a yellow complexion, such was the new viceroy, a fitting embodiment of the irritation and determination of the German governing class. The period of greatest tension since 1871 now began and lasted for several years, indeed all through this regency, which ended only with the promotion of Hohenlohe to the chancellorship of the Empire in 1894. It was a period of danger, replete with incidents that set Germany, France, and Alsace-Lorraine on edge. Boulangism, then in the ascendant in France, was seized upon by Bismarck for the classic purpose of bringing about an increase of the army and securing a freer hand for the imperial government by making it less dependent than ever upon parliament. Grossly exaggerating the alleged menace from France, Bismarck demanded additional troops and particularly demanded that the appropriations for the army be voted for a period of seven years, the famous Law of the Septennate. The Reichstag, quite naturally not wishing to alienate its powers for so long a period, to reduce its own importance, none too great at best, rejected the demands of the Iron Chancellor, January 14, 1887. Bismarck replied that very day by issuing a decrce dissolving the Reichstag, and by beginning throughout the Empire one of the most violent political campaigns in its history. By unabashed pressure upon the voters, by the unscrupulous exploitation of the "French menace" in order to inspire alarm, he won a crushing victory at the polls and quickly secured the Septennate. The Liberals and Socialists were routed and the Reichstag was weakened as a factor in the state, by this important diminution of its powers.

Meanwhile Hohenlohe had tried to use the war scare in Alsace to secure from the voters the election of candidates favorable to the project of the Chancellor. He told the Alsatians that, if war came, their province would inevitably be the theater of hostilities and would be fearfully harried by the contending armies. The result of his intervention was quite unexpected. All the Alsatian deputies opposed to the Septennate were reëlected by large majorities. Candidates patronized and supported by the Statthalter were decisively defeated. A solid delegation of fifteen "*protestataires*" was sent to the Reichstag. Of 314,000 registered voters, the "protesters" received 247,000 votes, that is 82,000 more than had been cast for them in 1884.

So stiff-necked a people needed emphatically to be tamed and tamed it should be. Bismarck went at the congenial task with determination, exceedingly irritated by the overwhelming condemnation of his policy in Alsace at the time it was so overwhelmingly approved throughout the Empire. Extraordinary, exceptional measures now rained upon the devoted heads of this independent people. The leading Alsatian minister, Hoffman, considered too mild for the work, was recalled and Puttkammer, a relative of Bismarck, was appointed in his place, and began at once a policy of punishment and repression. Puttkammer had declined even to accept his post, that of Secretary of State and President of the Ministry of Alsace-Lorraine until Antoine, deputy from Metz, and whose very name was an entire programme, according to Puttkammer, had been expelled from the Reichstag. Accordingly the Reichstag expelled him on March 31, 1887, an act entirely pleasing to those who did not care for parliamentary immunities. Against another deputy from Alsace, Lalance of Mulhouse, a decree of expulsion was issued, then suspended, then replaced by judicial prosecution and finally by a mere administrative measure, which forced the unwelcome deputy to depart.

A vigorous attack was made forthwith on various Alsatian organizations, art clubs, the medical society of Strasburg, botanical and zoölogical societies. Other organizations which refused to admit the German immigrants to their membership, such as gymnastic and choral and student clubs, were likewise dissolved by administrative decree. Whatever societies escaped annihilation were subjected to a Draconian régime, were obliged to submit their statutes to government officials for revision, and allow their banners and insignia to be examined so that the least French word might be stricken from them. They must also declare their willingness henceforth to admit to their membership the German immigrants. No French sign might be put over a store, no word of French might be used at a funeral, or find a place on a gravestone.

A series of incidents also occurred, alarming and calculated to increase the irritation and tension of the times, such as the brutal arrest, on Alsatian soil of Schnaebele, a French railway official at Pagny-sur-Moselle, by his German colleague of Novéant who had summoned him hither for the transaction of routine business, an incident that for several days caused all Europe to hold its breath (April 20, 1887). Later (September 24) a German forest-guard shot and killed one Frenchman and wounded another, who were peacefully hunting on French soil, at Vexaincourt, not on German soil. In June, 1887, eight Alsatians were tried before the Supreme Court at Leipsic for belonging to a League of Patriots and four of them were found guilty and were sentenced.

This policy of intimidation received its appropriate coronation in a measure, which, in the opinion of the German government would completely subdue the recalcitrants, a new and drastic regulation prescribing the use of passports, a measure put into force June 1, 1888. Henceforth certain categories of people were absolutely excluded from Alsace-Lorraine, for instance anyone connected with the French army. Every other person, not a German, who wished to enter Alsace-Lorraine must get a passport viséed at the German embassy in Paris, and it was intended that this passport should be granted only in exceptional cases. The purpose was to erect a Chinese wall between France and the annexed provinces. The theory behind this measure was that the reason why the Alsatians and Lorrainers had not hailed the Germans as deliverers and benefactors was that, though such was their inclination, they were terrorized from expressing it, not terrorized by the government to which they were now subject, with its dictatorship, its exceptional laws, its systematic espionage and the denunciations of its immigrant officials, who daily mailed their innuendoes and delations to Berlin.

The official German doctrine was that it was not the Germans who terrorized German Alsace. It was the French! It was through fear of the censure of their friends and relatives who had remained French, it was through fear of French public opinion, that the Alsatians rejected assimilation with the Germans!

No sooner was this Byzantine theory conceived by the authorities than it was adopted with enthusiasm by the journalists of Germany, for whom the ridiculous and the servile have no terrors.

To protect the Alsatians against intimidation by their French relatives, intercourse with persons beyond the frontier was made impossible, by the system of passports. This measure did not break their spirit, but it did harass them, and at times its cruelty was particularly inhuman as, for instance, when it prevented a son or daughter, resident in France, from going to a dying parent in Alsace-Lorraine.

Alsace, then, was as completely isolated from France as she could be. This was the famous "peace of the graveyard" and it continued for many years. As if this were not enough to make Germans loved in Alsace the Prince von Hohenlohe tactfully chose the French national holiday, July 14, 1888, as the occasion on which to announce at Mulhouse, that "other measures would follow designed in a durable way to detach Alsace-Lorraine from France and to attach her to Germany."

Even those Alsatians who had shown a tendency to go over to the side of the government were repelled by these senseless and cruel methods, declaring that they were well calculated to extinguish any tendencies toward reconciliation. But the system continued, and the death of William I, the accession of William II, the fall of Bismarck in 1890 made no difference. The new Chancellor, Caprivi, revealed clearly the purpose of the government when he said, on June 10, 1890, that he was resolved to maintain the system of the passports in order "to deepen the gulf which separated France from Germany." Caprivi added the significant confession, "It is a fact that after seventeen years of annexation, the German spirit has made no progress in Alsace."

Bismarck, before his fall, had shown his irritation

by talking of suppressing the Delegation and the representation of Alsace-Lorraine in the Reichstag, and of dividing the Reichsland between Prussia, Bavaria, and Baden, trusting these to absorb and destroy all reminders of a separate individuality and consciousness. There is even ground for believing that he favored for an ulterior reason all the oppressive measures carried out by Hohenlohe.

There is a significant passage in the *Memoirs* of Prince Hohenlohe, under date of May 8, 1888, which throws a flood of light upon the purpose of this policy: "Since last spring," writes the Statthalter, "in consequence of the excitement produced by the result of the elections, we have introduced a number of more or less vexatious measures, which have aroused much ill feeling. Prince Bismarck thereupon desired me to introduce the system of compulsory passports against France, which existing legislation allows me to do upon my own initiative. He informed me that our ambassador at Paris would not be allowed to *visé* any pass without previously asking permission, so that infinite delays would arise in consequence. There is no doubt that this measure would not only excite general surprise and excitement, but would also greatly embitter the local population. It seems that Berlin desires to introduce these irritating measures with the object of reducing the inhabitants of Alsace-Lorraine to despair and driving them to revolt, when it will be possible to say that the civil government is useless and that martial law must be proclaimed."

This would mean that the civil law would be suspended, that the summary process of courts-martial would represent the highest justice. In that case, also, the few concessions hitherto made to Alsace-Lorraine could be annulled.

This then was the culmination of twenty years of German rule in the conquered provinces. The passage quoted is a sufficient commentary on the statesmanship displayed by the government which knew better what was good for the people of Alsace-Lorraine than did the people themselves.

What the people thought of it, however, was shown in the elections of 1890. Alsace-Lorraine again sent a delegation largely of "protesters" to the Reichstag in Berlin.

CHAPTER VI

ALSACE–LORRAINE, 1890–1911

WE have traced the history of German rule in Alsace-Lorraine during the first twenty years of its existence. Month after month, year after year, the policy of repression was continued with a cold tenacity of purpose. In time it produced an effect. In 1890, four "non-protesters" were elected out of the delegation of fifteen to the Reichstag. The success of these four was due solely to the weariness and discouragement of the voters, and to their hope that if they voted for candidates agreeable to the government, then the government would loosen somewhat the fetters which were strangling them, would let in a little fresh air where all were suffocating.

The system of calculated and comprehensive terrorism, however, continued despite this virtual appeal for mercy. There was to be no premature leniency. The people of Alsace-Lorraine must repent and bring forth fruits meet for repentance. Convinced of the efficacy of their method, noticing signs of flinching on the part of their victims, the imperial authorities continued the policy of torture, moral if not physical. Owing to the operation of the passport régime the Alsatians lived, as it were, in a demi-vacuum, almost suffocated. Cut off from their friends in France, permitted to receive only those French newspapers which consented to forego all reference to them, their letters opened by an active *"Cabinet noir"* whose efficiency would have pleased even Metternich in the palmiest days of the European reaction, they saw one tie after another snapped that connected them with France, saw all fruitful and helpful communication with their true mother-country and with their relatives in France brought to an end.

As the years went by a new generation grew up which thus lost touch, so vital and so necessary, with France. Meanwhile the older generation which had known what it was to love France and to fight for her, which had kept the faith during all these years, was rapidly disappearing, gathered to its fathers in the final resting place. The new generation had had no other experience than that of German subjects. All its members had passed through the German schools, its young men had known service in the German army. Could they escape the powerful impress of institutions which had played upon them during their formative and critical years? The German officials in Alsace, considering themselves adepts in the subtle art of the psychology of peoples, relied confidently, in their reports to Berlin, on just these impalpable but inevitable changes of time. The stars in their courses were fighting for the cause of the Hohenzollerns. Time was on their side, for time brings with it a new understanding, new currents of ideas, new interests, a riper appreciation of realities, a juster sense of the possible and the impossible. Gods that at first seem strange and unsympathetic will in time come to be worshipped and old idols will be discarded when their impotence is manifest to all.

Therefore, let the transforming finger of time do its work. Meanwhile, however, let whatever mundane and specific devices there are for hastening the process be used by a wise government. Vigilance is the price of despotism as it is said to be the price of liberty. Consequently the German government encouraged and favored any measure that seemed likely to help in the work of dissociating and dispersing the Alsatians into various groups, of breaking up their solidarity, of strengthening new currents of thought which might divide and distract them. Thus Socialism, which was imported from Germany by the German workingmen who came in considerable numbers to Strasburg and Mulhouse, Socialism, fought tooth and nail elsewhere by the government, was here first tolerated by it, and then distinctly aided, when its divisive effect upon the public mind was seen. It would serve as a counter-irritant to the local aspirations and might also help to stalemate the liberal bourgeoisie of the cities and the great manufacturers who had supported the policy of protest.

Another agency for influencing opinion into governmental channels was seen in the upper stratum of the hierarchy of the Roman Catholic Church. Hitherto there had been no more effective leaders and spokesmen for the people in their repudiation of the Treaty of Frankfort and of the despotism it had fastened on the land than the Catholic clergy. Of the fifteen men first chosen to the Reichstag from Alsace and Lorraine, and who made the memorable protest of 1874, seven were ecclesiastics, two bishops, four parish priests and one abbé. One of the purest and bravest patriots of this people in captivity was Monseigneur Dupont des Loges, Bishop of Metz, whom nothing could buy or intimidate and who was a pillar of strength to a people in distress, distress of body and of soul, who was as the shadow of a great rock in a weary land. The lesson of his power was not lost upon the ruling class of Germany who only waited for the opportunity to lay their hands upon the high personnel of the Church in order to use it for their purposes. Intriguing with the Holy See when vacancies occurred, in 1899 and 1900, in the two bishoprics of Metz and Strasburg, the imperial government was successful in getting the two positions filled, not by Alsatians or Lorrainers, but by two Germans from Germany. Henceforth, the spiritual heads of the Church in the Reichsland were devoted henchmen of the powers that were, active agents in the work of Germanization. Some of the Catholic clergy refused to follow in this new orientation and adhered to the old line. But many did follow. Thus there was division where formerly there had been approximate unanimity in the Catholic world; as there was, also, through the spread of Socialism, division in the ranks of the working classes. Everything seemed, from the official point of view, to be working together for good, for the obliteration of the old groupings of the population into simple "protesters" and "non-protesters." New groupings were appearing, Catholics in Alsace-Lorraine working in union with Catholics in Germany through the agency of the Center party; Socialists of Alsace-Lorraine working together with the Socialists of Germany for the triumph of their cause. Old war-cries were being forgotten, new party alignments cutting across the old were drawing the Reichsland from its former moorings into the general currents of imperial politics. The particularism of Alsace-Lorraine, the irreconcilable states-rights feeling, was being sapped and mined by the new forces which were in the world contending for mastery. The separate personality of the annexed provinces, the product of their peculiar and highly individual history, was in danger of being absorbed and consequently annihilated in the Nirvana of Gross-Deutschland. The old ideals were apparently losing their power and new interests, religious or social or economic, were taking their place.

The chronology of this change cannot be given with exactitude. But symptoms of the change were apparent in 1890, and they became steadily more pronounced during the last decade of the nineteenth century. The government, while not yet satisfied, was quite content with the progress that was being made. The Alsatians might not love Germany, but they feared her and were proving amenable to the devices and practices of strong government. The policy of steady compulsion and compression, resumed in deadly earnestness after the slight dalliance with the decently humane conceptions of the "era of Manteuffel," was justifying itself. The only way to judge a tree is by its fruit and the bureaucrats of Berlin and their servile agents in Strasburg viewed the present with complacency and sensed a serener future. But the situation, during these years, was not quite so simple, after all.

The people of Alsace-Lorraine, harried by the hostile and drastic legislation which we have passed in review, treated with insolence by the immigrant Germans who came by the scores of thousands to fill the offices of the bureaucracy and to carry out its prescriptions with the thoroughness and the rigid adherence to tradition characteristic of the Prussian civil service, knew full well what it was to be a subject people. They had felt, year in year out, the heavy weight of the imperial government. They saw how powerless they were, how unequal any contest was with their masters who could and would at any moment, when they judged it necessary, let loose an overwhelming force to terrify and to crush. They saw clearly how tightly they were caught in the mesh of a despotic system. Indignant at an oppression unworthy of Europe in the nineteenth century, but none the less existent however ignoble, stunned by the régime of terror which brought only the forced "repose of the cemetery," seeing, as the years went by, less and less hope of liberation from outside and none from within, with every factor of the situation adding to the discouraging perspective, nevertheless they did not flinch but fought on with admirable loyalty to their traditions and with admirable courage.

The form of the contest changed, but the substance of it never changed from 1871 to 1914. Though the expression varied according to circumstances, the contest was always against the policy of Germanization which the conquering country was determined to effect. Rebellious to this from the very depths of its soul, Alsace was resolved that this should not be. Her opposition to the policy of Germanization has been the constant, unvarying feature of her history from 1870 to the present day.

At first, as we have seen, her opposition took the form of "protest" against the régime established by the Treaty of Frankfort, against annexation to a foreign country without her own consent, and in the teeth of her passionate denial of the right of conquest. In election after election for twenty years, she sent a solid delegation to the Reichstag of "protesters" against the odious deed. But the iniquity seemed inexpugnable as year after year went by. The victors went their way, tightening their grip more and more firmly.

In the last decade of the nineteenth century, Alsatian opposition to German rule assumed a different form. Realizing that they could accomplish nothing practical by ceaselessly protesting against the fact of annexation, which in truth only increased the rigors of the government, giving it new pretexts for oppression; at the same time resolved to block the avowed policy of Germanization, which aimed at assimilating them completely with their conquerors, at stamping them with the same impress, at making them over in the image of Prussians, the people of Alsace and Lorraine resorted to new methods which they were to continue to use down to the beginning of the present war. No longer continuing the policy of simple protest, as futile, recognizing the fact of annexation to the German Empire, without accepting it as a right, they now insisted that they should be given the privileges of Germans, that they should no longer be ruled as were Togo and

Cameroon by collective Germany, but that they should enjoy those powers of self-government which Bavarians, Würtembergers, and Saxons enjoyed. They should become an autonomous state, like the twenty-five states that made up the Empire. They asserted their right to be Germans *in their own way*, just as the Bavarians were, the right to make the local laws which affected their daily lives so intimately at every point that they ought to be the expression of their local wishes or idiosyncracies; and the right to have these laws administered by Alsatians and not by a horde of immigrant officials derived from everywhere in Germany except Alsace. " Alsace for the Alsatians" was the new cry. The Alsatians had, they asserted, the same right to govern themselves, and to express their personality, also the same right to share in the government of the Empire as a whole, as had the people of the other confederated states. As it was, they formed a mere province of the Empire, not controlling their own local affairs, but having them controlled by a combination of outsiders, Prussians, Bavarians, Saxons, Mecklenburgers, Brunswickers; and not participating in the control of national affairs. Though they had fifteen members in the Reichstag they had no voice in the Bundesrath, a far more important body. Their local

Delegation was a mere semblance of a local parliament, which did not even represent the people but was practically a semi-official body, a parliament, moreover, likely at any moment to be snubbed, ignored, or overruled by the imperial government. They demanded that the régime of exceptional legislation should cease and that they should be given a position in the Empire similar to that of the other states. Alsace-Lorraine must no longer have the status of a subject province. Complete statehood must be granted her. She must be recognized as the equal of every other German state, in independence, in rights and powers and privileges.

There was more in this demand than appears at first sight, more than the mere desire to escape from a degrading political tutelage, a position of glaring political inequality. There was a social and a national purpose to be subserved; namely, the preservation, the conscious preservation, of their own individuality, of their own civilization, which they knew and affirmed to be distinct from that of the other German states. Certainly it was outrageous and humiliating, to be at the mercy of officials who came from beyond the Rhine and this must cease. But it was even more important that Alsace and Lorraine should be able to preserve their own habits and customs, should be able to turn their own evolution in whatever direction they might wish, unhampered by external control.

Along with this political movement went an intellectual movement—both parts of the conception of Alsace for the Alsatians. The consciousness of their own separate individuality increased in clearness and intensity from this time forward until the great *débâcle* of 1914. The leaders of the movement felt that they were not weaving pretentious fancies, framing chimerical Utopias. They felt that they were grounded on the solid basis of the past history of their little corner of the world. Despite the immigration and the emigration of the period after 1870 yet the native element represented three fourths or more of the population and the intruding foreign element had not been able to modify the local character or mind. There had been no fusion of the new racial elements with the old, but only the juxtaposition or rather the superimposing of the new as masters of the old. The Alsatians and Lorrainers were not masters in their own house but others were the masters. This must be changed.

What was this *Alsatian individuality*, which the intellectuals insisted must be respected by Germany and must be given free opportunity for self-expression and for growth? Wherein did the Alsatians have any special originality? In what respect did they differ from the other Germans?

Bismarck, Moltke, Treitschke, Mommsen and the hierarchs of German politics and thought asserted that the Alsatians were pure and genuine Germans, and that that was all there was to it. Their tone of finality allowed no discussion. There might be a little French varnish on some of the élite, but it was a mere surface polish which would easily yield to treatment, either artificial treatment, that of the State, or natural treatment, that of time. The Alsatians were Germans, of German race, speaking the German language, who had lived for centuries in the German fatherland. What more was there to be said? Evidently nothing, by anyone who cared to be known as a sensible or intelligent human being.

The Alsatians, however, have had a good deal more to say about this interesting and, to them, vital topic. And their opinions illuminate a subject, in which not only the Pan-Germans are greatly interested but also the world in general. One has only to glance through the pages of the *Revue alsacienne illustrée*, a journal founded for the express purpose of giving voice to the Alsatians' sense of individuality, and ably conducted by Dr. Pierre Bucher, a citizen of Strasburg, to become aware of the lamentable superficialty and the fundamental falsity of official German utterances upon this important matter. Let us listen for a moment to native Alsatians commenting upon their country and themselves.

Alsace had had a history, and a long history, full of wars, full of vicissitudes, wars in which she was simply the battlefield used by the great powers in their struggles with each other, wars also in which she was herself an active participant, zealous to fight for the maintenance of her liberties. As a border land she had for two thousand years experienced the usual fortunes that fall to lands lying within an exposed and ambiguous zone. This varied and agitated experience had produced a local character, a local outlook upon the world, local aptitudes and inclinations and aspirations which differentiated her from other people. With much in common with them, she possessed much that was peculiar to herself. The elements which went to the making of the personality of Alsace were mingled in different proportions from those which prevailed in the making of other peoples. She spoke a German tongue, or rather, to speak more accurately her peasantry spoke various dialects of Germanic origin. But her bourgeoisie and her upper classes spoke French.

Her population was of Germanic origin, but so for that matter were the populations of large parts of Switzerland, the Netherlands, Great Britain, even Northern and Northeastern France. She had had an exceptional history and this had given her an identity of her own. Now that she was politically included in the German Empire was she just like the other German states, was she to be assimilated to a common type? Her originality in the confederation of German states consisted in precisely this, that her culture was not purely Germanic, but was mixed, compounded of German elements—and of French. The Germans repeated everlastingly the same refrain, that she had for eight hundred years been a part of Germany, and that this had made her German. They declined to admit that because she had for two tremendous centuries been a part of France she had become French. Yet as far as dynamic, formative influences were concerned the eighteenth and nineteenth centuries were far more important, far more transforming, far better adapted to leave a profound mark than the eight centuries that preceded them. In her thinking, in her political and social ideas and convictions and aspirations, in her whole feeling and way of looking at things she was French, and she was French because she had passed through the glow, the heat, the alembic of the French Revolution. In comparison with that experience, with its new and fiery evangel, with its radical and pervasive changes in institutions and ideas and sentiments, what was the long, rather sleepy, quite localized existence within the Holy Roman Empire? As experiences inevitably bound to impress a personality upon the people there could be no question that the two centuries of contact with France had contributed more to the making of modern Alsace than the eight centuries of contact with Germany—if there was a Germany—which had gone before. The one had accomplished the fusion of a people by its terrific heat, by its marvellous alchemy. The localized life within the rather unreal, unsubstantial Roman Empire had no such power as this to shape, to captivate, to transform. The one was a furnace that sent forth molten metal, the other a lumber room, a receptacle of all kinds of neglected survivals of the past.

German writers and rulers are prone to ignore these two centuries in the history of Alsace, and to hurry back to the time of the Hohenstauffen. The last two centuries are throbbing in the heart of Alsace to-day. The throbs emanating from the earlier period are few and far between. The Nibelungen and the Minnesinger leave her cold but the *Marseillaise* sets her tingling and vibrating with painful ecstasy. That the Germans knew the potency of the *Marseillaise* over the minds of the Alsatian people was shown by the fact that after 1871 they had forbidden the playing or singing of it. Yet this supreme revolutionary song, this battle hymn of freedom in every European land for a century, was in a real sense the product of this very Alsace. It had been composed in Strasburg, by Rouget de Lisle, at the request of the mayor who wanted a war song expressive of the revolutionary exaltation which he and his fellow citizens were experiencing. There is much instructive history in this single fact that the *Marseillaise* was composed and was played and sung for the first time in Alsace. But those who proclaim the fundamental Germanism of the Alsatians do well to ignore this fact and its implications, do well to pass lightly over the two centuries and to hark back to the medieval mummeries of the Holy Roman Empire.

But even that earlier history teaches a lesson, throws a certain light upon the development of Alsace not much insisted upon by German scholars and publicists, but which it is well to mention. The life which the Alsatians had lived as members of the medieval empire had been calculated to make them more sympathetic to modern France than to modern Germany, had not been at all calculated to make them good Germans in the sense in which that word was used by Bismarck at the close of the nineteenth century. The Alsatian of to-day is fundamentally republican and democratic and the beginning of this tendency is to be discovered early in Alsatian history. Down to the time of the annexation of the country to France, Alsace had never been a political entity. It had consisted of the "ten free cities" and of numerous petty principalities. All had had the right to govern themselves, if only they would give men and money to the far off Emperor in Vienna when he wanted them. Left largely alone, the Alsatians had had a practical independence and at least the beginnings of self-government. Never in their history had they known a national dynasty, as had Saxony, Bavaria, Brandenburg, Hesse, and innumerable other German states. The Alsatian has never known that adoration of the monarch and of monarchy, which is characteristic of the Prussian. With those initial popular tendencies confirmed and rendered more profound by the intimate connection with revolutionary France, the Alsatian is in his political ideals and connections poles asunder from his masters, the Prussians, with their veneration for monarchy, their respect for the social hierarchy, for authority. The German is a conservative, the Alsatian a democrat. The German accepts docilely inequality in the state, in society, in the army, and does not rebel against the gross privileges which birth or wealth gives in each of those spheres. The Alsatian, product of a different history, loves liberty and the equality of all before the law and hates arbitrary, despotic government and the reign of privilege.

In view of all this, what if he does speak German? If language is not fundamentally a mere set of sounds, if it is a set of ideas and emotions, then the Alsatian does not speak the same language as the Prussian. He does not feel that submissiveness to authority which is the prevalent and dubious distinction of the German; he does not care for all that has persisted in Germany of the Old Régime, that exaggerated regard for the national divinities, the State, the Kaiser, the nobility, the army officers, but on the other hand he sees the ridiculous in many of their pretensions and poses. The caricaturist, Hansi, is the truthful representative of this Alsatian irreverence and impatience.

In the production of the Alsatian of to-day the

period since 1789 has counted infinitely more than many previous centuries, just as it has in the production of the contemporary Frenchman.

The Alsatian mentality then, as formed and stamped by history, was of a very different type from the dominant mentality of Germany.

There was, consequently, little chance of mutual understanding, between Germany and Alsace-Lorraine, none whatever of sympathy. The peremptory psychologists of Berlin with their repetitious assertions as to the essential and complete identity of Germans and Alsatians were not accepted as authorities in Alsace. On the contrary the "intellectuals" of the Reichsland, knowing the history of their country and its effects, challenged the official doctrine, demanded that Germany respect the individuality of Alsace, and sought in various ways to impress upon the Alsatians themselves the menace to their heritage of ideas and customs involved in the imperial policy, and the necessity of their maintaining that heritage intact. The last quarter of a century has witnessed in Alsace the counterpart of what has been witnessed in other parts of Europe, a revival and intensification of the sense of local individuality, of what in Germany is called particularism. Some of these Alsatian intellectuals have worked in the field of the fine arts, painting, engraving, decoration, architecture, literature. Perhaps the most successful achievement has been the plays of Stosskopf, pieces written in Alsatian dialect, played by Alsatian actors, and portraying with psychological insight and with lambent humor and pungent satire the types and characters of contemporary Alsace.

Other "intellectuals" have found a congenial field in collaborating with Dr. Bucher, on the *Revue alsacienne illustrée,* studying the history, literature, art, and customs of Alsace. The *Revue* has been supplemented by lectures and pageants and festivals, given throughout the province, all aiming at a reinvigoration of the local consciousness, at the encouragement of the people to preserve their inheritance of culture in the face of the menace from Germany. Satire and caricature too, have contributed their part, in the work of Zislin of Mulhouse, and Hansi of Colmar, whose power has been evidenced by the fines and the terms of imprisonment with which they have been honored by the German courts.

All this intellectual movement helped the politicians in their campaign of Alsace for the Alsatians. This meant, as we have seen, that Alsace ought to have the right to make her own local laws, to enforce them through Alsatian officials, to be no longer at the mercy of the Bundesrath and the Reichstag, and of the German immigrant officials. It meant, too, that the attempts at Germanizing them, followed since 1871, and now asserted with increasing and arrogant emphasis by the Pan-Germanist party which was already in full swing, must cease. The Alsatians insisted that they be allowed to keep their spiritual and intellectual connection with France. Herein lay their originality, that they, a German state, had shared in the literature, the thought, the ideals, the culture of France. The attempt to cut them off from all their French recollections, to dig a deep gulf between them and France, to stamp out all the traditions and memories of the French connection, must be abandoned.

The Germans, seeing that the Alsatians no longer sent a solid flock of "protesters" to the Reichstag, that they were splitting up into different parties, Conservatives, Centrists, Radicals, and Socialists, each of which worked with its confrères in the corresponding German parties, believed, or affected to believe, that the process of Germanization was succeeding, and that with the advent of the third generation since 1870 the absorption of the province in the Fatherland would be complete and final. The "question of Alsace" was getting on famously toward a satisfactory solution. They at first even seemed to find no danger in this cry of Alsace for the Alsatians and to patronize the "legitimate" development of Alsatian particularism. But this approval was insincere and in the word "legitimate" lay an ominous mental reservation.

What were the results of this new direction of Alsatian energy? It may be said that they promised after all to be slight and in all likelihood would have been slight had it not been for the lack of wisdom of the German rulers, for their inveterate, autocratic conceptions of policy, which might be veiled for a moment but quickly reappeared.

In 1896, Jacques Preiss, a young lawyer of Colmar, and a leader of "Young Alsace" said in the Reichstag, of which he was a member: "Gentlemen, the people of Alsace-Lorraine protested in 1871. They protested through their representatives, specially elected for that purpose, against the annexation to Germany. This protest has not been withdrawn since, either in law, or in fact. . . . The assimilation, the Germanization of the country has not advanced a step to this day. . . . Fear dominates and poisons our political existence. The Government does not understand the people, and the people do not understand the Government. . . . History will say: 'The German Empire succeeded in conquering Alsace-Lorraine materially, but its administration did not know how to conquer her morally, did not know how to win the heart and soul of the people.'"

Preiss was right. History will undoubtedly say just that.

In 1894, the Prince of Hohenlohe abandoned the position of Statthalter to become Chancellor. He was succeeded by a distant relative, Prince Hermann von Hohenlohe-Langenburg, who was destined to hold the office for thirteen years but who did not take as active a part in the government as his predecessors had taken. Elections still continued to show the same dispersion of the voters among the different parties. Only Preiss, joined now by another of the figures who were to lead the gradually emerging party of "Young Alsace," Abbé Wetterlé, continued a policy of energetic, though strictly legal, opposition and criticism.

But the policy of systematic repression seemed nevertheless to be having its effect. The government, finally feeling sure of the complete subjection of the people, made a few concessions. The system of the passports was mitigated, and finally abolished, excepting as it affected the military; the censorship of the press was rendered a little less severe; and finally in 1902 the famous Article 10 of the Law of December 30, 1871 (the Dictatorship Article), was suppressed. The future was to prove that the suppression was not to leave the government without abundant weapons of repression and of tyranny, old French laws and old Prussian laws or ordinances, dating from the early and middle nineteenth century, amply sufficing to that end.

These concessions did not indicate an intention on the part of the government to abandon its programme of Germanization; but indicated rather its confidence that the complete Germanization, the final fusion of natives and immigrants, the thorough assimilation of the Reichsland with the Empire, were now assured. In entertaining this expectation that henceforth the sailing would be smooth and that the longed-for haven would soon be reached, the government was underestimating its own powers of blundering, its talent for reopening old sores. By its reckless playing with the Alsatian demands for larger liberties and then crudely disappointing them, by continuing and even intensifying its opposition to everything in Alsace that recalled France, the French language, French traditions, French souvenirs, by conduct which became increasingly dictatorial despite the abandonment of the Dictatorship Article of the Law of 1871, the government succeeded finally in arousing and alienating even those elements in the Alsatian population which were the most friendly to it. "The Germans themselves," as another has said, "thus reopened with a light heart the question of Alsace-Lorraine, aroused once more the public opinion of France, and finally wearied the long patience of Europe."

We have traced the rise of the particularistic movement, the increasing demand for genuine local self-government, for an equal status for Alsace-Lorraine with the other states of the German Empire. The number of those who looked forward to a return to France, either as a result of war or through some peaceful means, was small at the beginning of the twentieth century. Germany was so powerful and so resolute to keep what she had taken that the door of hope seemed closed and locked and barred. The protest in its original form was futile. Since they must live in the Empire, however, the Alsatians wished to live as comfortably and as freely as possible. This was the thought behind their demand for autonomy. They wished autonomy because it was the only régime worthy of grown men, the sole alternative being tutelage and subjection to others. They wished it also as enabling them to preserve the special character of Alsace-Lorraine, its liberty, its intellectual and spiritual contact with France, the most vital factor in its past.

This was entirely consistent with complete observance of the fundamental fact that they constituted a part of the German Empire. There was only one condition necessary, they must have as much freedom in the local life as had Bavaria and Baden, and the other twenty-three sisters in the confederation. All the Germans had to do was to give them this freedom, this opportunity to think and write and act, to preserve their traditions and their customs, to be themselves.

But Germany has never seriously thought of adopting such a policy. The dominant and constant idea in governing circles, political and military, has always been that force can accomplish anything it sets out to accomplish, and if not the present amount of force, then a still greater amount. As evidence of this temper Prince von Bülow's *Imperial Germany*, published in 1914, is enlightening, and particularly his treatment of subject peoples, like the Poles. However, in the twentieth century peoples are not content to be ruled as if they were regiments, their fate determined by arbitrary commands from above. Out of this divergence of views arose the final and complete rupture between the government of Berlin and its agents in Alsace on the one hand, and the people of the Reichsland on the other.

When the Germans pointed to what they had done for the province the Alsatians and Lorrainers asked: "Were they done for us," or was there another motive? Certainly the mileage of the railroads had been greatly increased since 1871, but much of this mileage was for military and strategic roads, leading nowhere except to the borders of France. Were these mammoth railroad stations primarily for the convenience of the civil population? Were not the elaborate means for handling big crowds, the spacious platforms, designed for another purpose, namely, the ease of entraining and detraining large bodies of troops? True, three million dollars and more had been spent for the buildings alone of the University of Strasburg, but the idea of the authorities in making these liberal appropriations was to have in the conquered territory a German university of the first rank, a center of the "German spirit," of "German science." In 1872 the University of Strasburg had 46 professors and 212 students; in 1900 it had 136 professors and 1169 students. In 1910, 175 professors. Yet it was and is a semi-foreign institution, not exercising the influence on the mentality of the Reichsland which had been intended. A significant fact, which also had an explanatory value, was that of the 175 members of the teaching staff in 1910, only fifteen were Alsatians. There is an illuminating phrase in a speech of Dubois-Raymond in Berlin in 1870, "The University of Berlin, housed (einquartiert) in a building opposite the Royal Palace, is the intellectual body-guard of the House of Hohenzollern." The Alsatians have had their doubts, which in our own day a large part of the world has come to share, about the desirability of such a bodyguard for such a House.

Again, among the works of architecture which the Germans had built in Alsace during the occupation there were too many barracks, too many Forts Moltke and Forts Crown-Prince. And why were the numbers of the troops stationed among them so large and why were they constantly increasing, 67,000 in 1890, 79,000 in 1895, 85,000 in 1909? Bismarck's brutal statement that Germany had not conquered Alsace-Lorraine for her good looks, her "*beaux yeux*," but as a "glacis," for purposes of national defense, had never been forgotten by the conquered.

In every aspect of the life of Alsace-Lorraine there had been more room for thought of the Alsatians and Lorrainers themselves than the imperial authorities had ever bestowed.

The growth of Alsatian particularism, which has been described, was met and challenged by the rise in the Empire of the Pan-German party, with its aggressive, chauvinistic, ultra-nationalistic programme. This party opposed the government bitterly for any concessions it thought of making or did make to the people of the Reichsland. Its members in the immigrant bureaucracy of Alsace-Lorraine fed the flames by their strident denunciations of conciliatory men and measures and by their incessant attacks upon France and everything French, consequently upon the natural and deep sympathies of the Alsatians, mindful of their indebtedness to French civilization, of their participation in the French spirit.

As an illustration of the tone and temper of German government in Alsace nearly forty years after the Franco-Prussian war, of its solicitude for local feeling, the official treatment of the language question may serve. France had never, during the period of her sovereignty, sought to impose her language upon Alsace, to the exclusion of German. While French was favored, German was not neglected. Both were taught in the primary schools and consequently those who had only the primary education had the opportunity to learn both languages.

Not such was the policy of Germany. One of her earliest measures, after the annexation, was to suppress the teaching of French in the primary schools, allowing it in the higher schools, though under conditions, even there, which did not encourage it. Later it abolished obligatory French in the normal schools. The results alarmed many Alsatians, becoming more and more vocal in demanding their rights, of which this would appear to be one of the primary and indefeasible ones. As a result a motion was made in 1908 in the Landesausschuss by M. Kübler, asking for obligatory instruction in French in the primary schools of Alsace-Lorraine. The reason given was an economic one, the practical utility for a border population to know both languages. The motion was passed by a practically unanimous vote. But above the Landesauschuss is the Government, that is the Statthalter, and the Alsatian Ministry; and above them is the Federal Council in Berlin, which has power to overrule anything they may do. In this case they did nothing. Consequently, Kübler, in March, 1909, asked what the Government proposed to do. The president of the ministry gave a reply that was unsatisfactory to the Landesauschuss, stating that the teaching personnel for obligatory French would be lacking and that there were regions in which French would be useless.

A more limited motion was then made to the effect that French should be taught in the primary schools of all localities whose municipal councils should ask for it. At once the municipal governments of the large cities pronounced themselves unanimously in favor of this motion. Finally on May 12, 1909, the ministry announced that it was not opposed, in principle, to the teaching of the French language, but that it ought not to be taught in the primary schools except in those localities near the frontier, that outside that area its teaching would be prejudicial to the general curriculum, would derange the plan of studies, that the pupils who were particularly capable could attend the higher grades, where they would have the opportunity desired.

The answer being unsatisfactory to Kübler and other members of the Landesauschuss, a special commission was appointed with Kübler as chairman and Abbé Wetterlé as secretary, to study the different propositions which had been submitted. This committee presented a report on July 6, 1909, which demanded that the government favor in every way the necessary instruction in the French language by absolutely requiring it at least four hours a week in the upper grades of the primary schools, by not restricting any more than in the other states of the empire private instruction in French by persons outside the teaching staff, by authorizing the teachers in the primary schools to teach French outside the class-room and without limiting the number of pupils, by authorizing communities to organize, outside the primary schools, instruction in French at their expense and under the supervision of the regular school authorities and by taking steps so that French should be taught sufficiently in the normal schools and should be required for graduation from them.

Motions designed to carry out these recommendations were passed unanimously. The whole affair aroused the passions of the country and gave rise to many incidents. Herr Gneisse, a director of a

Gymnasium in Colmar, was the spokesman of the Germanizers and protested against the motions; Hansi (J. J. Waltz) published a caricature of a German pedant, which Gneisse considered an allusion to himself. Hansi was prosecuted and fined 500 marks. The Abbé Wetterlé's name was brought into the case, whereupon Gneisse prosecuted Wetterlé. Preiss and Blumenthal, members of the Landesauschuss and Wetterlé's lawyers, thereupon called attention to the question which was at the bottom of the case—"namely, on the one hand the entire people and the Landesauschuss demanding this instruction, on the other hand, a clan of Pan-Germanists, Gneisse and consorts, opposing it." Wetterlé was condemned to two months in prison.

"Alsace-Lorraine," says an historian of this period, "will teach French when other wills than her own permit her to."

The spectacle of a nation which prides itself upon its exceptional enlightenment waging war in the twentieth century upon a language which is the mother tongue of twenty per cent of the population of Alsace, is unworthy as well as intolerable. It is also at times ridiculous. The German government permits no new business signs in the French language to be put up over stores. Consequently, old French signs, even when shabby and dilapidated, are retained by many firms, since to regild would mean the necessity of changing from French to German. *Dupont Frères* refuse to be Germanized into *Gebrüder Dupont*, and make it á point of honor and of local loyalty to maintain the old form in spite of a meddlesome bureaucracy. Now and then incidents arise, serio-comic in nature, in this fatuous war upon a language, conducted at the orders of the government of a people which does not question the superiority of its culture over that of all other peoples. A few years ago a shopkeeper was obliged to change his sign *Liquidation totale*, which is French, into *Totale Liquidation*, which is German. Administrative wisdom permits "Friseur" but forbids "Coiffeur." There have been historic struggles in Alsace as to whether the name inscribed in the register of births should be Jean, as desired by the parents, or *Johann* as desired by the authorities, whether René or Renatus.

The government, which has been capable of these achievements, a few years ago, before permitting the inauguration of a monument erected at Wissembourg by Alsatians in memory of Alsatians who had died upon that field in the Franco-Prussian war, demanded the removal of four emblems carved on the corners of the pedestal; the sun, emblem of Louis XIV, the lily of Louis XV, the axe and fasces of the Revolution, the eagle of Napoleon!

CHAPTER VII

THE CONSTITUTION OF 1911

THE people of Alsace-Lorraine had for forty years been in absolute subjection to other wills than their own. Though allowed a Delegation or Landesausschuss, before which routine legislative proposals were laid, yet that body was elected not directly by the people but indirectly and largely by and from district and municipal councils, so that, by reason of its complicated and carefully controlled composition as well as because of the humble character of its powers, it could only be servile. It could at any moment be overruled by outside powers, by the local executive, appointed from Berlin, or by Berlin itself. There was in this form of government no satisfaction given to the legitimate desire of the Alsatians to manage their own affairs. As the demand for local states-rights grew, as it enlisted the sympathies of the more liberal German parties and of many members of the Reichstag, who recognized that the Alsatians and Lorrainers were only asking for what they themselves had always had, and as the government felt that the grip of Germany upon the Reichsland had steadily increased with the lapse of time and was now unshakeable, it finally came to feel that it was safe to grant some of the concessions which were so greatly desired. On March 15, 1910, the Chancellor of the Empire, Bethmann-Hollweg, announced in the Reichstag that the Emperor had agreed with the confederated governments to grant a more autonomous constitution to Alsace-Lorraine. This announcement was received with lively satisfaction. But the people of the Reichsland were soon to learn that the Greeks are not the only people to suspect when they come forward bearing gifts. When, on June 29, the members of the Landesauschuss expressed the desire that the Landesauschuss should be consulted beforehand as to the constitutional changes under consideration in Berlin they were informed by the Alsatian ministry that the Imperial Government did not recognize the right of the Landesauschuss to mix in questions which belonged exclusively to the Bundesrath and the Reichstag.

Indeed the speech of the Chancellor ought to have checked any undue optimism on the part of the Alsatians. Stating that it was necessary to grant "a greater political independence to Alsace," the

Chancellor proceeded to lecture both the Pan-Germanists—for their opposition to any concessions—and those whom he called the "Pan-French," for their particularistic and Francophile agitation. The cry "Alsace for the Alsatians" had, he said, a seductive sound, but he added that this could never be realized as long as the leaders of the movement affected not to recognize the fundamentally German character of the population and aimed at Gallicising the country in the face of ethnography and history. This remark, divested of the Hegelian wrappings with which Bethmann-Hollweg was accustomed to clothe his thoughts, meant that the Alsatians must break the ties that bound them to the culture and civilization of France, and must immerse themselves exclusively in the culture and civilization of Germany. Only then could they expect to be treated as valued members of "the family of German states."

The cause of Alsace was thus really lost in advance. After this cold douche any clear mind could see what was likely to come. The actual plan for reform was not laid before the Reichstag until December, 1910. Its discussion dragged from the start. When the Landesauschuss expressed opposition to certain features of the plan, its session was abruptly closed, May 9, 1911, an action which naturally produced a bad impression upon the country. On May 26, 1911, the new Constitution of Alsace-Lorraine was voted by the Reichstag. Violently opposed by the Pan-Germanists and betrayed by those so-called liberal parties in the Reichstag whose supposed principles required that they support it, Alsatian autonomy came out practically by the same door wherein it went. Only one change of any importance was made. The Landesauschuss, or single-chambered body, was now to give way to a bicameral legislature which was henceforth to be the sole source of legislation for Alsace-Lorraine. The lower house was to be elected by secret and practically manhood suffrage but this house was to be balanced by an upper house in which the Government would always be assured of a majority. The control of the legislature over the budget, a vital test of its importance, was affirmed but was rendered illusory by the provision that if it should refuse to vote it, then the Government should be entirely free to levy taxes and incur expenses on the basis of the preceding budget, that is, to raise and spend as much money as ever.

Moreover the legislature, in this respect like the other legislatures of Germany, would have no means of enforcing its wishes. The executive power remained concentrated, as before, in the hands of the Statthalter who would reside, it is true, in Strasburg, but whose inspiration and instructions would come, as hitherto, from Berlin. The local ministry was to be, as hitherto, responsible not to the elected chamber, but to the Statthalter alone, and the Statthalter was responsible only to the Emperor. As the Statthalter and the ministry were to appoint and control the bureaucracy, or civil service, Alsace would remain, as in the past, entirely subject to an oligarchy of foreign officials, the detested immigrants from Germany, and to the daily vexations and irritations of a despotic bureaucracy. Every individual in Alsace would be subjected as during the past forty years to the system of espionage which is one of the ubiquitous elements of modern German government. The infamous rôle of the informer, which the Alsatians had hoped to stamp out by themselves getting control of the administration, would flourish as before.

The Constitution of 1911 pretended to raise Alsace-Lorraine to the rank of a German state, to place it on a plane of equality with the other twenty-five members of the confederation. In practice it did nothing of the kind. It allowed her three votes in the Bundesrath. She would thus, like all the other states, be represented in both the Bundesrath and the Reichstag. But the three delegates from Alsace-Lorraine were to receive their instructions from the Statthalter, were to vote in the Bundesrath as he might direct. But the Statthalter was not an independent sovereign like the King of Saxony or the Duke of Mecklenburg, ruling by his own right; nor was he an elected republican head of the state. He was appointed by the Emperor, and was his representative, revocable at will and consequently not likely to do anything distasteful to him. The Constitution of 1911 increased greatly the power of the Emperor; it did not increase the power of the people. In theory Alsace-Lorraine was given statehood; in practice, she was to be as tightly bound as ever.

In short the new Constitution was a fraud, as is so much in the "constitutional" guarantees of contemporary Germany, whether in the nation or in the individual states. Moreover, into the Constitution itself were written miserable and vexatious prescriptions limiting the use of the French language in Alsace-Lorraine.

To mock a people's aspirations in so crude a manner was a practical joke, of doubtful taste. The Alsatians were shown, in all this campaign of much talk about nothing, that nowhere in Germany did they have any friends in their desire for real self-government, not even in the Center and Socialist parties which decisively betrayed their allies in the Reichsland for the sake of the immediate political advantages which offered themselves. The latter coöperated with the Conservatives and the Pan-Germanists in granting this mockery of autonomy. The trail of Pan-Germanism was everywhere to be seen in the annexed provinces during the few remaining years of peace.

The new Constitution was not, therefore, of a character to arouse much optimism or gratitude in Alsace-Lorraine. Moreover, there was, to anticipate a famous phrase, no assurance that it would be more than a scrap of paper. A constitution granted from on high, it might at any moment be withdrawn by those who granted it, if they should become dissatisfied with its working or annoyed with the people who were the recipients of the benefaction.

It was indeed provided by Article 28 that any further modification of the new Constitution should be made by the Reichstag and the Bundesrath. The people themselves of the new "state" would not be able to change their fundamental law in any particular. Their Constitution of 1911, like that of

1879, now superseded, was blighted in the same way. Its life was extremely precarious. At any moment the legislative organs of the German Empire were at liberty to withdraw it or to alter it. Alsace-Lorraine remained what she had always been in theory and in fact, an Imperial Territory, a Reichsland, the property of the collective states of the confederation. She was bound hand and foot to the executive and legislative powers of Berlin.

The people of Alsace and Lorraine were thus checked, and completely balked. Great was their disillusionment. The hope for real self-government in place of degrading tutelage, legitimate for any intelligent people in this day and age, a hope at times encouraged by imperial politicians for tactical purposes, was now brutally dissipated. Among the enemies who stood across the pathway of their aspirations the most energetic and bitter were the Pan-Germanists whose influence was increasing every day and who were giving a sharper tone to German policy and one of increasing menace to the world. The catastrophe of to-day is the logical and natural outcome of their vigilant, contemptuous, and aggressive spirit. Proud of its military and naval power, entertaining the most vaulting ambitions which could only be realized at the expense of others, modern Germany was riding gaily for a dazzling triumph—or for a fall.

The repercussion of this Pan-German movement was felt widely throughout the world, in France, in England, in the Balkans. It was also decidedly felt in the conquered provinces. Pan-Germanism fundamentally means conquest by arms. It was in the provinces so conquered in 1870 that the military preparations attained the highest pitch of intensity. The signs of the times were unmistakable.

The period from 1911 to 1914 was the last act in the long and ignoble history of oppression which since 1870 has been the sign manual of German rule. The situation became steadily more and more critical for the Alsatians and Lorrainers. Among the German immigrant office-holders in the Reichsland were many Pan-Germans, the bitterest opponents of every proposition to grant autonomy, to try conciliation with the people of the provinces, indignant at the resistance to the policy of Germanization on the part of these renegade sons of the Fatherland. For the Pan-Germans, within Alsace and without, if chastising with whips did not suffice, then chastising with scorpions should be tried. There comes a moment when the rebellious spirit, apparently the most intractable, recognizes its master and submits.

After 1911 a species of terrorization was organized in Alsace-Lorraine. Spies infested the country, denouncing every manifestation of opposition or criticism. Even local officials like the Statthalter, Wedel, or the chief secretary, Zorn von Bulach, a native Alsatian who had long ago gone over to the German official side, were reproached bitterly by this aggressive and uncompromising party with lukewarmness and indifference to the welfare of the Fatherland, whereas an outsider would have had difficulty in finding any pronounced mildness or regard for popular feelings in their acts. They could, however, tell the difference between the practicable and the flagrantly unreasonable. Informed and sensible men like Werner Wittich, a German professor at the University of Strasburg, seeking to enlighten public opinion throughout the Empire on the real situation in Alsace and recommending a liberal and tolerant policy, were overwhelmed by the clamor of the Pan-Germanists.

During the three years preceding the present war the cloven hoof appeared repeatedly. The public opinion of the provinces was exacerbated and alarmed by a series of irritating episodes which showed the people the humiliation of their position, the fragility, indeed the non-existence, of any guarantee of their liberties. Hansi (J. J. Waltz), a native Alsatian, was thrown into prison, as we have seen, for having caricatured a Pan-German high school teacher, Herr Gneisse, and in 1914 he was, to the stupefaction of the world, prosecuted for high treason in the federal court at Leipsic because of caricatures which in any self-governing country would pass current as the most ordinary satires upon the foibles and pretensions of the official class. Abbé Wetterlé, editor of a newspaper in Colmar, and formerly a member of the Reichstag, was condemned to fine and imprisonment for protesting against the insolence of the Pan-Germans. A merchant of Mulhouse was expelled from Alsace for having asked a hotel orchestra to play the *Marseillaise*. During these years, also, the authorities proceeded against numerous Alsatian societies and clubs in a way that could only create widespread irritation and resentment, against choral unions, gymnastic clubs, and societies founded for the purpose of caring for the graves of Alsatians who had died on Alsatian soil during the Franco-German war.

In addition to military and political pressure, economic pressure was also used to further the programme of Germanization. Alsatian economic interests were repeatedly sacrificed in the interest of neighboring states like Baden or of the powerful Rhenish-Westphalian steel- and iron-mongers. Alsatian manufacturers or merchants were the victims of despicable informers and all who were suspected of French sympathies were made to feel the full displeasure of the government. The great locomotive corporation of Graffenstaden, on which the life of that town absolutely depended, was informed that there would be no more government contracts, unless it dismissed a manager whom the Pan-Germanists considered Francophile. As the business would have been ruined without government orders, the deed was done. The Alsatians were made to understand the significance of the economic boycott practiced against themselves by their own government, a government which now denounces as an outrage the very thought on the part of the Allies of using this weapon against itself.

The reaction of all these incidents, grave or petty as the case might be, was exactly what might have been expected. The Alsatians and Lorrainers united as one man against this recrudescence of tyranny. Dropping their differences of opinion, ignoring party lines, they joined in indignant protest against a government which subjected them to continued maltreatment, which failed to assure them the most elementary rights of free men. The hollowness and the mockery of the boasted Constitution of 1911 were patent to all the world in the light of these events. It was not the Alsatians, not the French, who were chiefly responsible for the fact that forty years of German rule had not brought peace or reconciliation. The chief cause was the character of that rule itself, which every year kept alive popular discontent and which was now accentuating it more and more by renewed disclosure of the gulf that lay between the governors and the governed. The Germans might have learned from old or recent English history the healing and invigorating quality that lies in liberal treatment of a conquered people. The history of Canada and of South Africa would have proved instructive. But as Balzac said many years ago: "There is one instrument the Germans have never learned to play. That instrument is liberty." It is the Germans who are responsible for the question of Alsace-Lorraine not only in its inception but in its progress and fruition. Denying categorically that any such question exists, they have made it one of the danger spots of modern Europe and through their handling of it have given the world the accurate measure of their ability and character as rulers. The fate of Alsace-Lorraine is a striking and melancholy object lesson to a world threatened with German domination. The history of Alsace-Lorraine is a sufficient revelation of what such a domination would mean.

CHAPTER VIII

THE SAVERNE AFFAIR

The German system of arbitrary and oppressive government was appropriately crowned, a few months before the outbreak of the present war, by the incident of Saverne. The whole philosophy and practice of the contemporary German state was vividly revealed in that affair. The German method of treating the conquered and the feeling of the conquered for Germany were seen to have undergone no softening change with the lapse of forty years. The original protest of 1871 was no more emphatic than the outburst of indignation aroused in Alsace-Lorraine, and in every class of society, by this new and culminating outrage. The Treaty of Frankfort, the Saverne Affair, these are the Alpha and the Omega, the beginning and the end of modern German statecraft.

Saverne, or Zabern, as the Germans call it, is an Alsatian town of about nine thousand inhabitants located in the foothills of the Vosges. It was to be made famous in 1913 by the actions of a young officer, callow and conceited beyond the permissible limits of any age. Lieutenant Baron von Forstner was twenty years old, was a native of East Prussia and exemplified in his personality the qualities of the Junker class, of whose blood and breeding he was a typical illustration. He called the Alsatian recruits whom he was training by an opprobrious term "Wackes" or rowdies, ruffians. He told his soldiers to use their weapons fearlessly if they should come into collision with the local civilians and offered a prize of ten marks to anyone who should succeed in "sticking" any Alsatian native who should assault him. His under-officer, similarly valiant, took occasion to say that he himself would add three marks out of his own pocket to any such hero. Forstner's insults to the Alsatian recruits were frequent. He went so far as to oblige them to say, when presenting themselves to him, "I am a Wacke."

These things became noised abroad outside the barracks and naturally aroused indignation. These wanton insults were levelled, it was felt, not at individual recruits, but at the people of Alsace. But the people kept their self-control under provocation as they have kept it steadily since 1871. "We are Alsatian Wackes," cried some street gamins to

THE SAVERNE AFFAIR

the Lieutenant as he walked through the town. Others trailed along after him saying to each other in their salty dialect: "Say, tell me, you, how much is an Alsatian Wacke worth?" "Why, ten marks, of course." Laughed at and teased by the people, especially the children, Forstner gave up walking alone. Whenever he appeared he was escorted by a patrol of four soldiers who stood with bayonets fixed before the shops where he bought his chocolates and cigars. Going to a restaurant he placed a loaded revolver by his plate and with surpassing imbecility stabbed the bill of fare with his sword because he saw on it the French word "*poularde.*" This, of course, incited the natives to renewed laughter and sarcasms.

In spite of, or perhaps because of, the growing agitation of the town, Lieutenant von Forstner thought fit to crown his work by showing his contempt for France as well as for the Alsatians, using an expression of defilement concerning the French flag. The use of the gross and vile term was flagrantly unprofessional, as well as indecent, and was against all army etiquette and tradition, formal respect toward the armies and officers and flags of other nations being taught as a military virtue in all the armies of the civilized world. Such language as that used by Forstner, in Alsace of all countries, with its traditions, was a deliberate provocation, a cut across the face.

The colonel of the regiment, von Reutter, instead of suppressing this firebrand of a petty officer, supported him and proceeded to give the world his own measure. Complaining about insufficient protection on the part of the local authorities, he took the law into his own hands. He served ball cartridges to his soldiers, had machine guns got in readiness, cleared the public squares, and threatened to fire upon the crowd in front of the barracks, if they did not disperse. They did.

Not only was all Alsace trembling with resentment at the gratuitous insults and the arrogance of the officers, not only were public meetings held to protest against these acts, but when the Reichstag met on November 25, 1913, a debate was precipitated on the incidents of Saverne. The Minister of War, General von Falkenhayn, declared from the tribune that the utterances of Lieutenant von Forstner did not constitute insults because "he had not the least idea that his words would become known to the public." Falkenhayn reserved all his wrath for those soldiers who had divulged them and had thus, as he said, committed a gross offense against "one of the elementary conditions of discipline in the army."

The attitude of the army officers was being rapidly outlined. High and low, from lieutenant to Prussian Minister of War, all thought alike. With such a temper in military circles, naturally dangerous incidents continued to occur. On the evening of November 28, at seven o'clock Lieutenant von Forstner, in company with some of his comrades, was seen in a public square by some gamins who forthwith proceeded to jeer and taunt him. Lieutenant Schadt rushed to the barracks to warn the guards who, eighty strong, came out. Colonel von Reutter placed himself at their head and there began a veritable man hunt. Twenty-nine persons were arrested, some for having laughed, others for not moving on, others for having moved on too rapidly. Some were arrested even in their houses the doors of which were broken down by the soldiers. Among the men thus rounded up were the prosecuting attorney and three judges of the local court who were on their way home from the court house and who were apprehended because they protested against the illegal actions of the military. The men arrested were kept in a dirty dungeon, the coal bunker of the barracks, over night.

Had all this been opera bouffe, it would have convulsed the house. But it was not opera bouffe. It was German government in operation in the twentieth century. Not even local government, but national. The affair was no longer purely Alsatian. Colonel von Reutter, by covering the actions of his subaltern and by substituting himself for the police in a deliberate and offensive fashion, had raised in an aggravated form the dangerous problem of the relations of the civil and military authorities.

Public opinion was aroused throughout Germany. "We get the impression," wrote the military editor of the "Berliner Tageblatt," himself an officer, Commandant Moraht, "that behind this formidable display of military force there is concealed an entirely different purpose from that of merely chastising some street urchins. The question arises, is not this an attempt on the part of the military to play a bad turn upon the civil government of the Empire."

The Alsatian ministry sent an investigator to the scene of trouble; the sub-prefect or Kreisdirektor also intervened. But Colonel von Reutter went right on. Three new arrests were made by the military on the night of November 30.

An excellent way of pouring oil on the fire. Public

opinion grew more vehement. "This is the greatest scandal we have ever known," said the radical *Morgen Post*. "At Zabern, judges and public prosecutors are imprisoned but Herr von Forstner is at liberty; his imprisonment is not even contemplated, for, accompanied by four soldiers with fixed bayonets, he goes chocolate-buying. There are sights, more beautiful, more impressive, more grandiose than that of a Prussian lieutenant, accompanied by four armed soldiers, buying chocolate. We have already had the history of Captain von Koepenick. That affair was as ridiculous as it could be, but this history of the lieutenant of Zabern is more so—and the ridiculousness of it falls on Germany. This is why it is revolting and profoundly humiliating for the patriotic German."

The patriotic German was, however, destined to further humiliations. On December 3, representatives of Alsace-Lorraine in the Reichstag presented to that body the protests of the Reichsland against these deeds. The Emperor was absent from Berlin, hunting at Donaueschingen, as at the time of the *Daily Telegraph* incident in 1908, and did not consider it his duty to return to his capital. Bethmann-Hollweg, who had gone to him to get his orders, made a speech minimizing the whole affair and, like the Minister of War, blaming the soldiers who had told of the provocative remarks of Forstner. But the Reichstag was not disposed to let this question of the conflict of military and civil powers be thus cavalierly treated, and pressed the Chancellor hard. Bethmann-Hollweg declared that Forstner would be punished but declined to say what the nature of the punishment would be. As a matter of fact the Chancellor was as completely without power or authority in the matter as any private citizen. For the control of the army is the ruler's prerogative and his acts, in this sphere, do not require the countersignature of any minister. He is absolute. This is a fundamental feature of the Prussian monarchy. The army is the King's, not Parliament's. The civil authorities are powerless to prevent the encroachments of the military authorities. Bethmann-Hollweg was only a civil official.

"This is a confession of bankruptcy," exclaimed the Socialist Ledebour. As a matter of fact, such was the situation in Germany, the Army was a state within the state. The Reichstag now had one more opportunity to learn its own impotence. Not only did the Chancellor indicate his impotence and theirs but the Minister of War, Falkenhayn, peremptorily and in cutting language refused to make any statements in regard to the facts on the ground that as Minister of War he had no cognizance of them.

Mirabeau's famous phrase was being vindicated again; "Prussia is not a country which possesses an army, it is an army which possesses a country."

So indignant was the Reichstag at the high-handed actions of the military, at the impersonal, detached, and essentially trivial speech of the Chancellor, and at the flaming eulogy of the Prussian officers and army as defenders of Throne and Fatherland by Falkenhayn that it was in no mood to be put off. "The words of the Chancellor," cried Fehrenbach, a member of the Center party, "seem to come from another world. (Repeated applause.) Army officers are subject to the law. They are not nor ought they to be beyond its reach. That would be the end of Germany, *finis Germaniæ*. . . . We hope that the utterances of the Minister of War are not the echo of conversations which he has recently had at Donaueschingen. (Frantic and prolonged applause from the Center and the Socialists.) If that were so, then it would be a terrible blow for the Empire. (Thunderous applause.) Those who act thus fail to understand the responsibility which they are assuming at this time."

On December 4, Bethmann-Hollweg made another speech in order to calm the Reichstag. But that body refused to be calmed. In the midst of indescribable tumult it passed a motion censuring the Chancellor by 293 votes against 54, the former representing 10,200,000 voters, the latter 1,800,000.

Only the Junker Conservatives opposed the motion which ran as follows: "The Chancellor has treated the affairs concerning the interpolations relative to the incidents of Zabern in a manner which is not in agreement with the sentiment of the Reichstag."

This censure was levelled at the Chancellor, not for any acts of his administration—for the incidents of Zabern were deeds of the military—but because he had not been able to arrest the encroachments of the army officers. But the highest military authority in the army is, as has been said, the King of Prussia, an authority subject by the laws of Prussia to no control whatever. He could be reached only very indirectly.

However, here for the first time was a question, originating in Alsace and concerning Alsace, whose glaring implications were of interest to all Germany, which might now contemplate the nature of her liberties, the character of her government. What had been brought home to the Alsatians for forty years was now being brought home to the sixty million Germans who had eagerly coöperated in the work of oppressing Alsace and were now reaping an appropriate reward. The impotence of the Reichstag to control or seriously influence the course of the German Government was to be shown even more clearly on this occasion than it had been five years earlier in the crisis arising out of the *Daily Telegraph* interview.

On December 9, 1913, Bethmann-Hollweg stated that he had no intention of resigning because of the vote of censure. Members have mentioned the usage in France. "But even children know the difference between France and Germany. I know that there are people working to establish similar institutions here. I shall oppose them with all my might." Bethmann-Hollweg took occasion a little later to express the same idea even more pungently in the Upper House of the Prussian Landtag when he said that "votes of censure merely established the fact of a difference of opinion in a particular case between the Reichstag and the Imperial Chancellor."

The Reichstag was condemned in high places— and quite properly as it was quite impotent and would always remain so unless it were willing to fight for respectable rights as have parliaments in other nations. This it has never even seriously considered doing.

Meanwhile the doughty Lieutenant von Forstner was doing what he could to help along the humiliation of the civil authorities of the Empire and to emphasize the supremacy of the military. On the 2d of December, on the very eve of the first discussion in the Reichstag he had covered himself with new glory. While passing through the town of Dettwiller, a few miles from Saverne, at the head of a detachment of troops, he heard the familiar gibes of the people. Immediately the soldiers were ordered to chase the crowd and soon came back, bringing with them as prisoner a lame cobbler, named Blanck. As Blanck protested his innocence and sought to get free, Forstner slashed him across the forehead with his sabre, inflicting a severe wound. Not only was the cobbler lame, but he was being held by both arms by soldiers at the very moment of the valorous slash.

It seemed as if such an act must be condemned by the military authorities themselves in the interest of the good name of the army. As a matter of fact the Lieutenant-Baron was condemned, December 19, by a court-martial to 43 days' imprisonment, the minimum penalty possible under the circumstances, and hardly a serious satisfaction for public opinion. Forstner appealed. It would have been well to let things rest there. But worse was yet to come.

The military party now entered aggressively and audaciously upon the scene, apparently resolved to test this matter once for all, and to teach the German people their exact position in the sorry scheme of things. Colonel von Reutter declared himself responsible, stating that he had insistently recommended his subalterns to use their arms in order to punish any who should insult the German uniform; in particular he had ordered Lieutenant von Forstner not to go out without his pistol and to have his sabre always ready for use. It was now rumored that the Colonel would himself be sent before a war council.

Soon another theatrical incident occurred. On December 22, the head of the police of Berlin, von Jagow, a civil official subordinate, of course, to the Chancellor, published an open letter in the *Kreuzzeitung*, in which he criticised the condemnation of Forstner. "Military exercises are acts of state," he said. "Those who try to impede acts of state are liable to be prosecuted and punished. Consequently, Lieutenant von Forstner could not be placed on trial and still less be punished. The military court which condemned him has apparently failed to be guided by these considerations. If the law stood differently, its prompt amendment would be needed. For, if German officers who are garrisoned in what is practically the enemy's country, are in danger of being prosecuted for illegal detention because they endeavor to make room for the exercise of the power of the State, the highest profession in the land is disgraced."

Thus the Berlin prefect of police used his power to influence public opinion while the matter was *sub judice*. His impertinence and incorrection were flagrant. He explained with dubious casuistry that he was speaking not as prefect of police but as a doctor of law.

The Crown Prince now appeared upon the stage, judging the moment propitious. Telegrams sent by him to Reutter were published—telegrams of congratulation and including the famous phrase, "Go it strong." (Immer feste darauf.)

Would the Chancellor allow his subordinate, the prefect of police, to pass unrebuked? Would the Emperor neglect to notice the action of his offspring?

On January 5, 1914, at Strasburg, the capital

law, not force. This principle, applied practically to international affairs, meant that in the case of annexations or transfers of territory, the important thing was not the territory, but the population living in it, and that the wishes of that population must be ascertained and carried out.

This new democratic and humane principle was not a mere theoretical abstraction in 1871, not a mere iridescent dream. It was the recognized principle, controlling action on the continent of Europe in the great territorial changes of the period. It was a working principle—except in Germany. The Kingdom of Italy was based upon it. In 1859, 1860, 1866 and 1870, the peoples of the various Italian states voted, and by tremendous majorities, in favor of union with Piedmont. In 1860, Savoy and Nice were annexed to France only after the formal and overwhelming approval of the people concerned. By the plebiscite of April 22, 1860, 130,533 votes approved out of 130,839 cast, the total number of registered voters being 135,449.

The annexations of Prussia in 1866, on the other hand, were based upon the old principle of force alone. Hanover, Nassau, Hesse-Cassel, Frankfort and Schleswig-Holstein were annexed, without consultation of the people, by right of conquest. But even Prussia made a slight concession to the spirit of the times. By the Treaty of Prague of 1866, a treaty between Prussia and Austria, it was provided that the people of northern Schleswig (who were Danes) should have the right to vote as to whether they would become Prussians or remain within the Danish kingdom. Twelve years later the two contracting parties agreed to annul this article of the treaty and the popular consultation has never been held. Prussia and Austria have kept themselves untainted from the principle of the rights of the people to be consulted as to their fate.

Thus in 1871 two principles confronted each other, the old, feudal principle of the right of force, the new, democratic principle of the right of the governed. Either one might have been made the basis of the Treaty of Frankfort. Two eras stood confronting each other, the past and the future, two peoples, two mentalities.

It was a solemn and decisive moment, a turning point in history. Had Germany fallen into line with the rest of the world, had she consented that a plebiscite of the people of Alsace-Lorraine should determine whether they should henceforth be citizens of Germany or of France, then the new principle would have triumphed definitely in the world and Europe would have been a safer place in which to live.

But Germany, without a moment's hesitation, decided that her might gave her the right to Alsace-Lorraine and she took them, never for an instant admitting that the people concerned had any rights which she was bound to respect. She sided with the good old fossil past. The right of conquest, said Marshal Moltke with confidence, is "in conformity with the order of things established by God." That being the case, what is there to discuss? The wise man does not attempt to alter the decrees of the Eternal.

The Franco-German war produced in Germany an illimitable faith in force. The Prussianization of German thought, which our own unhappy days have revealed as so complete, began at that time. The most elaborate, systematic and potent anti-social, anti-humanitarian doctrine that Europe has known, enjoyed great prestige and authority, because it could point to successes of the most palpable sort. Germans believed that brute force could do anything and everything, and was entitled to do so. Also they came to imagine that this force would always be theirs and that other nations would never have it in the same degree, that as Germany had conquered France in 1871 so she could conquer others henceforth forevermore, a perilous conceit. A state of mind, of soul, was created that was black with menace for the world. The German spirit, victorious and inflated, was now open to those influences which have resulted in the monstrous tragedy of to-day, the boundless egotism, the inability to see that other nations have rights quite as sacred as those of Germany, the constant hostility to all attempts to improve the international relations of the world by the spirit of coöperation, of peaceful adjustment of such difficulties as arise, the concentration of the national attention upon war and warlike preparations, as if war were the only constant and stable and permanent social fact. "As long as men exist," said William II at Carlsruhe in September, 1909, "there will be those who are jealous and hostile. We must be protected from their attacks; this is why there will always be dangers of war and we must be ready for everything." Bethmann-Hollweg, on March 30, 1911, added an appendant to this Imperial thought: "Whoever thinks seriously and practically of the question of disarmament . . . must be convinced that this question is insoluble, as long as men remain men and states states."

CONCLUSION

Such is the sterile political monism of modern Germany, a philosophy that was not beyond the imaginative grasp of the cave-dweller's mind.

The conquest of Alsace checked the march of European civilization. No doubt great technical and economic progress has been achieved since 1871, but still greater progress would have been realized had the Treaty of Frankfort never been signed. The future of democracy was imperilled, the ultimate liberties of the world were rendered far more difficult of achievement by the militarism now enthroned in Europe.

Marshal Moltke said in 1870 that Germany would have to remain armed for fifty years to preserve her conquest but that then the Alsatians would have become patriotic Germans and would no longer desire to get free from their new fatherland. The fifty years of militarism have had quite other results.

Truer than the prophecy of the Prussian Field Marshal was the prophecy of a Catholic bishop. Monsignor Freppel said to William I in February, 1871: "Believe a bishop who tells you in the presence of God and with his hand upon his heart, 'Alsace will never belong to you.'"

What of the future? Ought Alsace and Lorraine to be returned to France? The Treaty of Frankfort has been torn up, not by action of France, which has never accepted it as morally binding but has scrupulously observed it as a fact, but by Germany herself which has steadily announced it as final and as "settling" the question of Alsace-Lorraine once and for all. For forty years and more German rulers and German generals have denounced France as ceaselessly meditating and plotting revenge. Whenever the governing authorities have desired to extract additional millions from the German people for the army, they have pointed to the alleged menace in the West, the irreconcilable foe, weeping for her children and refusing to be comforted. The Germans have never explained why the French must after forty years regard the Treaty of Frankfort as final when they themselves did not regard the Treaty of Westphalia as final although it had run two hundred and thirty-three years. German argumentation, however, is generally unilateral.

The war which the Germans have declared for a generation was coming from the West, has come, but not by act of France. It has come from "peaceful, God-fearing" Germany, and was conceived in Berlin and Essen. The Treaty of Frankfort was thrown into the waste paper basket along with another famous scrap in August, 1914.

CONCLUSION

When the future peace is made the first article in the territorial readjustment should be one restoring Belgium to the Belgians, and restoring to France her lost provinces, those lost in 1870 as those lost in 1914. No honest man believes that because Germany has controlled a tenth of France for the past three years she has the slightest right to that territory or ever will have or ever could have. If she should keep her grip upon them for forty years and more, as she has kept it upon Alsace-Lorraine, she would have no greater right than on the very first day of her unspeakable aggression. There is no more a question of Alsace-Lorraine to-day, after forty-six years of occupation, than there is a question of the Department of the North, after three years of occupation.

If the German annexations of 1870 are justified, then the actual annexations of the present war are justified. The two cases stand upon an absolute parity. The people of Alsace and Lorraine have never admitted the right, they have only admitted the fact, of German rule, as no doubt the peasants of Northern France have done and are perforce doing at the present moment.

Ought there to be a referendum? No one would think of demanding that a popular vote should be taken to-day in the Department of the North, for instance, to see if it should become French again. There is no more reason for consulting the departments of Upper Rhine, of Lower Rhine, and of the Moselle, taken forty-three years ago, by precisely the same methods.

If the proposition had actually been realized which was made in 1917 by the German Foreign Secretary to the Mexican government that, for services to be rendered Germany by Mexico and Japan by their waging war upon the United States, Mexico should be rewarded by the acquisition of Texas, New Mexico, and Arizona, does any sane person believe that the people of the United States or the people of the states concerned would after forty years have consented to submit the question of their return to the United States to a popular vote, conducted by the Mexican government?

The practical difficulties in the way of a referendum arise from the initial act of violence. Who would be the citizens of Alsace-Lorraine entitled to vote and to decide by their vote the fate of the provinces? Should they be only the present residents? But over four hundred thousand Alsatians and Lorrainers have, owing to the annexation, left their native country without hope of return, and have kept their love of it undimmed in the bitterness of exile, of poignant separation from friends and relatives. Are they and their sons who have paid this heavy price for their fidelity to the fundamental principle in which every true American believes and must believe because it is the very corner-stone of our national independence and freedom, are these people to have nothing to say at the time when the reunion of their provinces with France is among the possibilities, and are the Germanizing agents and immigrants in Alsace to have the vote in such a plebiscite? Again, who would conduct the referendum? In view of the ruthless régime of murder, imprisonment, espionage, and delation which Germany installed in the provinces in August, 1914, would a referendum conducted under German authority be apt to be honest and scrupulous?

This issue does not admit of compromise. It must be kept as clear-cut as it is in its essential nature. The principle at the basis of the Treaty of Frankfort must be repudiated and emphatically discredited by its complete and resounding reversal. Never at any time since 1870 has Alsace-Lorraine admitted that it was German. It declared the Treaty of Frankfort null and void and it has never rescinded that declaration.

The character of the German government for forty-three years, the very provisions of German legislation during all these years, the measures of the German administration, the occasional admissions of German officials as to the real situation, all show conclusively that the official affirmation that Alsace-Lorraine has become thoroughly German has not been believed even in the official circles which have made the affirmation. Their conduct has belied their words. Has German policy in Alsace-Lorraine at any time since 1870 been based upon the theory that a people who admittedly were opposed to annexation have become reconciled to it and are loyal Germans? What has Germany done to turn hatred into love, dissatisfaction into contentment? Friedrich Naumann has admitted in his recent book, *Central Europe* "that the modern Germans almost everywhere in the world are unfortunately bad Germanizers." There is no more notorious commonplace in European politics than the egregious failure of the Germans to Germanize, or even to conciliate. Germany's Polish, Danish, French subjects are eloquent witnesses to this incapacity. Germany can hold people in subjection, she cannot or will not give them freedom. If the positive historical evidence which has been abundantly presented in the course of this narrative as to the feeling of the people of Alsace-Lorraine toward their conquerors had been entirely lacking, the most elementary common sense would have sufficed to show that no people could ever be won by such processes. Whatever material prosperity, whatever economic development has come under German rule, has made no difference to the public mind. Feelings of justice have a far deeper influence upon men than material considerations. The Alsatians have been held in slavery, for what is slavery if not subjection to the will of another? To be incorporated in a nation they detested, to be obliged to serve in its armies, and eventually to fight against those whom they consider their brothers, such has been the fate of the people of Alsace and Lorraine. If that be not slavery, what is it?

The twentieth century must redress the greatest iniquity of the nineteenth. The only action in harmony with justice and the rights of peoples is the return to France of the occupied provinces; those occupied three years ago and those occupied forty-six years ago.

The message of the modern world should be so emphatic, should be so free of all dubiety, should be so clear and loud, that it will penetrate the ears of all its creatures, even those who appear to be stone deaf. There should be no plebiscite. It must never be admitted that might can change a condition of right by creating a new right; that might may, if applied skilfully and ruthlessly, become right; that a territory may be annexed by might against its will; that the conqueror may then send scores of thousands of his subjects into it to settle, may at the same time drive from it scores of thousands of its natives and may for forty years try to terrify and corrupt those who remain, and that then the sum total of all these high-handed acts of violence alters the situation. In the interest of clear thinking and honorable, humane action, this notion must be stamped out. Otherwise we shall admit that time and the continuous use of oppressive methods suffice to make valid a monstrous iniquity. If the passage of time can alter the character of a crime, then robbery is legitimatized after a period, then persecution, if extended over years enough, and if vigorous enough, is morally justified by its results. The moral sense of the world will never be content with any such sophistical method of enabling the robber to become the permanent beneficiary of his crime.

In the coming work of European reconstruction the lamentable injustice of 1870 must be repaired.

The Protest of Bordeaux must be shown to be more august and valid in the conscience of mankind than the Treaty of Frankfort. No single act could secure so emphatically for conscience the position that belongs to it in the affairs of the world and before the tribunal of history.

It may at times have seemed that the question of Alsace-Lorraine was a dispute concerning only France and Germany. The world, if it has ever thought so, now knows better. There can be no excuse for ignorance as to its significance. This is blazoned forth in letters of fire upon every page of contemporary history. From 1871 date the arrogance, the conceit, the sense of invincibility of the Germans, the conviction that Providence has raised them up to be the leaders of the world and that nothing can fail which they set themselves to do, sentiments which have grown steadily to appalling proportions and have finally attained their legitimate expression in the wanton attack upon the liberties of the world. The words of the deputies of Alsace and Lorraine uttered in the Assembly at Bordeaux on February 17, 1871, were true and singularly prescient, a poignant prophecy, every letter of which has been fulfilled or is in rapid process of fulfillment:

"Europe cannot permit or ratify the abandonment of Alsace and Lorraine. The civilized nations, as guardians of justice and national rights, cannot remain indifferent to the fate of their neighbors, under pain of becoming, in their turn, victims of the outrages which they have tolerated. Modern Europe cannot allow a people to be seized like a herd of cattle; she cannot continue deaf to the repeated protests of threatened nationalities; she owes it to her instinct of self-preservation to forbid such abuses of power. She knows, too, that the unity of France is now, as in the past, a guarantee of the general order of the world, a barrier against the spirit of conquest and invasion. Peace concluded at the price of a cession of territory could be nothing but a costly truce, and not a final peace."

A world which has had militarism imposed upon it and a universal war let loose as a result of the intoxication of pride and the lust of power of Germany is in a position to appreciate the pitiless accuracy of this forecast of 1871. Upon it is incumbent the redressing of a monstrous wrong in a manner so unqualified and so emphatic that in the future no aggressive power will be tempted to repeat the evil deed.

It has been suggested that Alsace-Lorraine be

made an independent and autonomous monarchy with a royal house of her own, within the German Empire. It has also been suggested that she be made an independent and neutralized state outside the German Empire as well as outside France. These are but ways of evading the problem, not ways of repairing a grievous wrong which has been and still is a serious public injury, an offense to the world's sense of justice, and a menace to the world's peace. They ignore the rights and the wishes of the people concerned. The wrong can be repaired in only one way, by the return of these provinces to France where they belong and where they desire to be.

It should be a source of pride for Americans to know that they may aid in the vindication of right and justice, of liberty and humanity. Alsace-Lorraine is a symbol as well as a fact. She represents the cause of the oppressed everywhere. She has come to personify the momentous controversy which has been going on in the world for the past one hundred and forty years since the American and the French Revolutions challenged the principle of force as the authoritative arbiter in human affairs and asserted that the people have the right to determine their allegiance, that they must be consulted and obeyed by the governments, that they are no longer chattels to be passed from hand to hand as the result of battles or campaigns. The closing eighteenth century saw a war begin between peoples and kings. That war has continued intermittently ever since. It has entered, it is to be hoped, upon the last and final stage. Either the old religion of force is destined to be immensely revitalized and is to hold the field free of competitors, or the modern religion of the rights of peoples is to win the day.

It was appropriate, as it was inevitable, that, unless the people of the United States were to be recreant to their country's ideals and indifferent to its interests, they should have a place in the present stage of this epochal controversy as they had in its beginning in the eighteenth century.

As our soldiers and our sailors steam down the harbor of New York on their way to the field of battle they pass the statue of "Liberty Enlightening the World," the work of a gifted son of Alsace, Auguste Bartholdi, of Colmar. Under that prophetic and inspiring sign they go forth to fight the good fight for freedom.

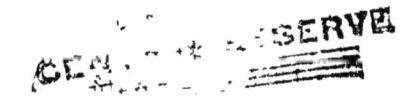

INDEX

INDEX

Allamans, 25
Alsace
  Annexation to Germany, 5, 6
  Attachment to France, 52
  Cession to France 1648, 39–41
  Diversity, 32
  Earliest history, 30, 31
  Early civilization, 34
  Early wars, 33, 34
  French Revolution in, 52–63
  Incorporation with France, 41, 42
  Individuality, 150, 151, 153, 158
  Isolation from France, 136
  New generation, 140
  "Alsace for the Alsatians," 148, 161, 177
Alsace-Lorraine
  Annexation, Germany's reasons, 78–96
  Before the treaty of Frankfort, 20–77
  Constitution of German Empire introduced 1874, 115
  France's policy from acquisition to the Revolution, 44–47
  From 1815 to 1870, 69–77
  Government, 1871–1890, 138
  Government, 1890–1911, 139–174
  New policy superseding protestation, 147
  People's service, 12
  Protest of people March 1, 1871, 13–15
  Protest of the people to the Reichstag, Feb. 18, 1874, 15–18
  Protests, 104, 116, 146, 195
  Since the Revolution, 63
  Transformation in the 18th century, 48, 49
Alsatian generals, 62, 64, 66
Angers, David d', 71
Annexation to Germany, reasons, 78–96
Annexations, 219, 225
Antoine, of Metz, 132
Arc de Triomphe, 64
Arizona, 226
Army, 120, 121
  Control, 196, 197
  Honor, 211
  See also Military authorities
Army officers, 193, 197, 198, 205
Arndt, Moritz, 67, 88, 89
Assembly, French National, 3, 4, 5, 12, 13
Austria, 36, 37, 79, 82, 89
  Prussia and, 220
Austria-Hungary, 83
Autonomy, 165, 178, 181

Back, 121
Baden, 32, 109, 165, 186, 210
Baden, Grand Duke of, 88
Balzac, 187
Bar, Duchy of, 33
Barracks, 167
Bartholdi, Auguste, 234

Basques, 80
Bavaria, 109, 156, 165, 210
"*Beaux yeux*," 119, 168
Bebel, 19
Becker, 89
Belfort, 5
Belgians, 12
Belgium, 79, 82, 101, 225
Benefactions, 105
Berlin, 6, 15, 182, 224
    Protest of 1874, 104
Berlin, University of, 92
    Hohenzollerns and, 167
Berliner Tageblatt, 194, 207
Bethmann-Hollweg, 176, 177, 195, 196, 197, 199, 214
    Censure, 198
    Quoted, 222
Biedermann, Charles, 90
Bischwiller, 103
Bismarck, 3, 73, 86, 91, 95, 106, 110, 118, 119, 128, 136, 137, 151, 168, 216, 217
    Boulangism and, 130
    Vigorous policy, 132
Black Forest, 84
Blanc, Louis, 4
Blanck, 200
"Blood and iron," 73, 96, 105
Blücher, 89
Blumenthal, 172
Bluntschli, Professor, 17
Bordeaux, 5, 231
    Protest of 1871, 104
Border states, 34, 152
Borny, 74
Boulangism, 130
Boundaries, 83, 120, 213, 214
Bourbon, House of, 36, 37
    Overthrow, 60
Boycott, 186
Brachycephalic skulls, 79

Brandenburg, 156
Bretons, 80
Briey, 86, 87
Bucher, Pierre, 151, 159
Budget, 178
Bulach, Zorn von, 184
Bülow, Prince von, 165
Bundesrath, 112, 113, 115, 116, 117, 118, 148, 179, 180
Bureaucracy, 125, 127, 145, 179
Business signs, 172-173

Cabinet noir, 140
Cæsar, Julius, 21
Calker, Professor von, 208
Canada, 109, 187
Caprivi, 136
Caricatures, 157, 185
Carlsbad Decrees, 70
Carlsruhe, 222
Catholic clergy, 142
    Germanization, 143
Catholicism, 36
Cavour, 106
Celtic race, 21, 84
Censorship of the press, 163
Central Europe, 210, 228
Centrists, 144, 160, 181, 197
"Chambers of reunion," 42
Chambord, treaty of, 38
Chancellor, German, 111, 116
Charlemagne, 25, 101
Charles V, 38
Charles X, 70
Christianity, 23, 25
Church
    German use of, 143
    Legislation affecting, 56
    See also Catholicism; Clergy
Cities, free, 32, 41, 67, 122, 156
Civil authorities and military, 194, 196, 209, 211

INDEX

Civil Constitution of the Clergy, 56, 57
Clergy
  Catholic, 142, 143
  Civil Constitution of the, 56, 57
Coal mines, 86
Cobbler, 200, 204
Coercion, 129
Coiffeur, 173
Colmar, 32, 159, 161, 172, 185, 234
Concessions, 163, 176
Concordat, 64
Conscience, liberty of, 39
Conservatives, 160, 181
Constitution of Alsace-Lorraine (1879), 116, 117, 118
Constitution of 1911, 175-188
Coulanges, Fustel de, 62
Counter-revolution, 57, 95
Courtesy, 119, 123
Court-Martial, 202-205
Crécy, 34
Crown Prince, 202, 205
Custine, 66

Daily Telegraph, 195, 199, 208
Dallwitz, 206, 212
Danes, 82, 220
Danish war, 73
Danube, 23
Decapolis, 32, 67
Delahache, Georges, 88, 99
Delegation. *See* Landesauschuss
Democracy, 11, 122, 156, 157, 223
  German, 209, 214
  Principle, 219, 220
Denmark, 101
Despotism, 115, 118, 145-146
Dettwiller, 200
Dictatorship Article, 113, 117, 163, 164
Dietrich, Mayor, 55

Disarmament, 222
Discipline, 106-107
Dolichocephalic skulls, 78
Donaueschingen, 195, 197
Dubois-Raymond, 167
Dupont des Loges, Monseigneur, 142
Dupont Frères, 173
Duty, 102

Eccard, M., 103
Economic pressure, 185-186
Edict of Nantes, 37
Education, 121
Eighteenth century changes, 48, 49
Elbeuf, 103
Emblems, removal, 173-174
Emigration, 98-99, 103-104
Emperor of Rome, 26
England, 79, 81, 89, 109
Equality, 157
Espionage, 179, 184, 227
Essen, 224
Ethnography, 78, 79
Ettenheim, 57
European politics, 216
Exodus of 1872, 98-99, 103-104

Falkenhayn, General von, 192, 196, 197, 214
Favre, Jules, 217
Fehrenbach, 197
Ferrières, 217
Feudal fiefs, 58
Feudal principle, 219, 220
Feudalism, 28, 29, 48, 58, 59
Figaro, Le, 7
Flag, French, 191
Fleckenstein, 32
Flemish language, 82
Force, 73, 105-106, 165, 214, 217, 219, 220, 221, 233

Forstner, Lieut. Baron von, 190, 191, 192, 193, 195, 196, 200, 201, 202, 204, 207
Foy, General, 70
France, 26
  Catholic, 37
  Changes in the 18th century, 49
  Dismemberment begun, 67
  Extension to the east, 37, 38
  Incorporation of Alsace, 41, 42
  Modern, 60, 213
  Policy with Alsace and Lorraine, 44, 45
  Title to Alsace, 40
  Unity, 35, 232
Franche-Comté, 88
Franco-German war, 3, 74, 221
Frankfort, 106
Frankfort, treaty of, 3–19, 87, 189, 219, 224, 227
  Alsace-Lorraine before, 20–77
  Consequences, 215–234
  One privilege of Alsace-Lorraine, 97
  Turning point in history, 220
Frankfurter Zeitung, 18
Franks, 25
Frederick Charles, Prince, 7, 8
Frederick the Great, 101, 109
  Quoted, 78
Frederick William III, 73
Free imperial cities, 32, 41, 67, 122, 156
Freedom. *See* Liberty
French language, 47, 180
  Attacks on, 133
  Study, 121
  Teaching, 169–172
French National Assembly, 3, 4, 5, 12, 13
French Revolution, 52–63, 154, 218

Alsace's peculiar relation to, 58–63
Military service, 61, 62
Freppel, Monsignor, 223
Friedrichs, 208
Friseur, 173

Gambetta, 4
Gaul, 22
Generals, Alsatian, 62, 64, 66
German Empire
  Constitution, 112
  Constitution and Alsace-Lorraine, 115
  Middle Ages, 26, 27
German Emperor, 180, 195, 207
  See also William II
German immigration, 145
German language, 47, 48, 80, 121
German princes, 30, 117
  Protest to Diet, 1789, 59
German spirit, 167, 222
German states, 112–113, 148, 149
Germanization, 102, 108, 121, 141, 160, 161, 163, 183, 186, 214
  German failure, 228
Germany
  Alsace-Lorraine position, 6, 7, 8
  Ambitions, 67, 68
  Feudalism, 28, 29
  Hatred of France, 72
  Liberalism, 72
  National thought and feeling, 93–96
  Pre-bellum, 93–95
  Subjects, 228
  Unity, 217, 218
  See Government
Gneisse, Herr, 171, 172, 185
"Go it strong," 202

INDEX

Government
  German method, 1871-1890, 108-138
  Temper of Germany, 168-169, 183, 187, 188, 228
Graffenstaden, 186
Gravelotte, 74
Gustavus Adolphus, 38
Gutenberg, 71

Hague Conferences, 216
Haguenau, 32
Hanover, 106, 219
Hansi (J. J. Waltz), 157, 159, 172, 185
Hapsburgs, 27, 32, 36, 37, 39, 40, 85, 88, 112
Hegira of 1872, 98-99, 103-104
Henry II, 38
Hertzog, 118, 125
Hesse, 106, 156
Hesse-Cassel, 219
Hesse-Darmstadt, Landgrave of, 58
"Historical rights," 84
Hoffman, 132
Hohenlohe-Langenburg, Prince Hermann, 162
Hohenlohe-Schillingsfurst, Prince Chlodwig von, 130-137, 162
  Memoirs quoted, 137
Hohenstauffen, 27, 154
Hohenzollerns, 27, 112, 141, 167
Holland, 79, 82, 84, 101
Holy Roman Empire, 26, 27-29, 34, 35, 84, 112, 154, 155
Holy Roman German Empire, 26, 29
Huguenots, 36
Humanity, 11

Imperial Germany, 165

Individuality, 113, 150, 151, 153, 158
Insults, 192
Intellectual movement, 150, 158, 159
Intimidation, 134, 135
Iron mines, 67, 86
Italy, 26, 106, 216, 219

Jagow, Herr von, 201, 202, 205
Japan, 226
Jean or *Johann*, 173
Joan of Arc, 34
Johann or *Jean*, 173
Josephine, 66
Judges, 100
Junkers, 190, 205
Justice, 211, 229, 230, 233

Kaiser. *See* German Emperor
Kayserberg, 32
Kellermann, 62, 66
Kings, 234
Kirschleger, 91
Kléber, 62
  Monument, 71
  Quoted, 65, 66
Koepenick, Captain von, 195
Kreuzzeitung, 201
Kübler, M., 169, 170, 171

Lalance, of Mulhouse, 132
Lamprecht, 214
Landau, 67
Landesauschuss, 116, 117, 118, 123, 175-178
Landtag, 199, 212
Language question
  German policy, 169
  See also French language; Linguistic theory
League of Patriots, 134

Leszcynski, Stanislaus, 43, 44
Ledebour, 196
Lefebvre, 65, 66
Legislation, 178
  Religious, 56
Legislature. *See* Landesauschuss
Leipsic, 134, 185
Leopold II, 59
Levetzow, Herr von, 7
Liberty, 157, 165, 187, 211, 213, 218, 234
Liberty of conscience, 39
Lichtenberger, 122
Liebknecht, 19
Lindau, 32
Linguistic theory, 80-84
Liquidation totale, 173
Lisle, Rouget de, 54, 155
Livonia, 79
Locomotive corporation, 186
Lorraine
  Annexation to Germany, 5, 6
  Earliest history, 30, 31
  Early civilization, 34
  Early history, 33, 34
  Language, 44
Lorraine, Duchy of, 33, 43
Louis XIII, 39, 101
Louis XIV, 39, 41, 84, 101, 104
  Strasburg seizure, 42, 43
Louis XV, 43, 47
Louis XVIII, 70, 89
Louis Philippe, 70
Lower Alsace, 111
Luxemburg, 88
Luxemburg affair, 91

Machtfrage, 109
Manteuffel, Field Marshal von, 123-130
Map "with the green border," 6, 88

Marseillaise, 54, 55, 155, 185
Mars-la-Tour, 74
Maurenbrecher, William, 93
Maurice of Saxony, 38
Mazarin, 39
Mentality, 158
Merlin of Douai, 59
Metternich, 70, 73, 109
Metz, 22, 33, 38, 74, 82, 86, 94, 132
  German intrigue for bishopric, 143
Metz, Bishop of, 142
Metz, Toul, and Verdun, 38, 43
Meuse, 88
Mexico, 226
Middle Ages, 24
Middle-Europe, 210, 228
Militarism, 211, 215, 223
Military authorities and civil authorities, 194, 196, 209, 211
Military reasons, 86
Military service, 120
Mines, 86
Mirabeau, 197
Modern France. *See* France
Moltke, 86, 90, 151, 223
Mommsen, Theodore, 63, 93, 151
Monarchy, 156, 157
Montesquieu, 50
Monument, emblems on, 173-174
Moraht, Commandant, 194
Morgen Post, 195
Moselle, 88
Mulhouse, 32, 36, 122, 132, 159, 185
  Curriculum of school, 121
  Incorporation in France, 43
Munster, 32, 36

Nancy, 44
Nantes, Edict of, 37

INDEX

Napoleon, 26, 29, 63, 64, 66, 69
Napoleon III, 73
Nassau, 219
National rights, 232, 233
Nationalism, 213
Nationality, 20
Naumann, Friedrich, 210, 228
"Necklace Cardinal," 57
Netherlands, 88
Neutralization, 94
New Mexico, 226
Ney, Marshal, 66
Nice, 106, 219
Ninety-three professors, the, 93
"Non-protesters," 139
Novéant, 133

Obernai, 32
Officials, 100, 101
Oldenburg, Herr von, 205
Oppression, 183
Organizations, attacks on, 133, 185
Originality, 151, 153, 160

Pagny-sur-Moselle, 133
Palatinate, 32
Pan-French, 177
Pan-Germanism, 82-83, 85, 93, 181, 183
Pan-Germanists, 160, 168, 172, 177, 178, 181, 182, 184
Paris, 52, 54, 64
Paris, second treaty of (1815), 67
Particularism, 158
Particularistic movement, 150-164, 168
Passports, 134, 135, 136, 137, 140, 163
Peace, 232
"Peace of the graveyard," 136
Philosophy, eighteenth century, 49, 50

Phrygian cap, 54
Piedmont, 219
Plebiscite, 97, 106, 219, 220, 225, 226, 227, 230
Poland, 9
Poles, 79, 82, 166
Police, 109
Polish refugees, 71
Popular rights, 11
  See also Rights
Portugal, 79
Poularde, 191
Prague, 85
Prague, treaty of, 220
Preiss, Jacques, 161, 162, 172
Presidencies, 111
President-Superior, 111, 113, 116
Privilege, victim's. *See* Victim's privilege
Professors, the ninety-three, 93
Protest to the National Assembly, 13-15
Protest to the Reichstag, 15-18
Protestantism, 35, 36
"Protesters," 128, 131, 138, 147
Protests, 104, 116, 123, 146, 195
Prussia, 67, 79, 81, 82, 89, 109, 211
  Annexations, 219
  Army and, 197
  Austria and, 220
  Policy, 105-106
  Rise, 73
Prussia, King of, 110, 111
  Army, 196, 198
Prussianization, 221
Prussians
  Courtesy, 119
  Creating, 105
Public opinion, 212, 213
Puttkammer, 132

Quinet, Edgar, 4

INDEX

Racial lines, 78–80
Radicals, 160
Railroad mileage, 166
Rapp, 66
Reason, temper of, 57
Recruiting, 120
Red Eagle, 205
Referendum. *See* Plebiscite
Reformation, 35, 36
Reichsland, 110, 111, 115
Reichstag, 15, 18, 111, 115, 116, 118
    Constitution of 1911 voted, 178
    Impotence, 196, 199, 209
    Saverne affair and, 192, 198, 199
Religious wars, 36
Renan, 84
René or *Renatus*, 173
Representation, 116
Republic, French, 60
Restoration, 70
"Resuming," 84, 85
Reubell, 51
Reuss, Rodolphe, 62
Reutter, Colonel von, 192, 193, 194, 201, 203, 204, 205, 207
Revue alsacienne illustrée, 151, 159
Rheinischer Merkur, 68
Rhine, 21, 22, 67, 83, 88, 90, 213, 214
Ribeaupierre, 32
Richelieu, 39
Richepanse, 66
Rickert, 68
Riga, 79
Right, 230
Rights, 200
    National, 232, 234
    People's, 97
Rights of men, 218, 220
Rohan, Duke of, 57
Roman civilization, 22, 24

Roman Empire, 25
"Roman Peace," 22
Rome, 26
Rosheim, 32
Rousseau, 50
Rupture, 166
Russia, 79, 83, 89

Saar, 67, 88
Saarlouis, 67
Saverne (Zabern), 22, 189
Saverne affair, 189–214
Savoy, 106, 219
Saxony, 156
Schadt, Lieutenant, 193, 203, 204
Scharnhorst, General, 95
Schlestadt, 32
Schleswig, 82, 220
Schlesweg-Holstein, 106, 219
Schnaebele, 133
School teachers, 100–101
Schools, 120, 121
    See also French language; Language question
Schramm, General, 66
Schroeder, Pastor, 96
Scotland, 79
Scrap of paper, 181, 224
Search, right of, 114
Ségur, Count de, 66
Self-government, 117, 182
    Movement for, 147–148
    See also Autonomy
Septennate, Law of the, 130, 131
Signs, business, 172–173
Skulls, dolichocephalic and brachycephalic, 78, 79
Slavery, 16, 112, 115, 229
Slavs, 25, 82
Socialism aided by Germany, 142
Socialists, 160, 181, 197, 209
    Alsace-Lorraine question and, 19

INDEX

Societies. *See* Organizations
"Song of Shame," 68
South Africa, 187
Sovereignty vs. territory, 41
Spain, 36
Speyer, 91
Speyer, bishop of, 32, 58
Spicheren, 74
Spies, 184
  See also Espionage
Statecraft, German, 189
Statehood, 179, 180
  Appeal for, 148-149
States-General, 51
Statthalter, 116, 117, 123, 179, 180
Stoeber, 68
Stosskopf, 159
Strasburg, 22, 32, 36, 71, 91, 122, 123, 124, 155, 179, 213
  Address (1790) to National Assembly, 55, 56
  Court-martial, 202, 205
  Franco-German war, 74-77
  German intrigue for bishopric, 143
  Mayor, 121, 122
  Revolution and, 54
  Seizure by Louis XIV in 1681, 42
Strasburg, University of, 91
  Germanization, 166-167
Strasburg Cathedral, 54, 57, 75-77
Subject peoples, 166
Subjection, 212, 228
Swedes, 38
Switzerland, 79, 81, 82, 84, 101

Temple Neuf, 75
Temple of Reason, 57
Territory vs. sovereignty, 41
Terrorization policy, 75, 76, 134, 135, 184
Teutonic invasions, 23

Teutonic race, 22, 24
Texas, 226
Thirty Years War, 37, 38
Toul, 22, 33, 38
  See also Metz, Toul, and Verdun
Treaties, 218
  List, 10
Treaty of Frankfort. *See* Frankfort, treaty of
Treaty of Westphalia. *See* Westphalia, treaty of
Treitschke, 104, 111, 112, 151
Tricolor, 54
Troops, 167
Turkheim, 32
Tyranny, 186, 188

United States, 81, 226, 233, 234
Universities of Strasburg and Berlin, 91-93
Upper Alsace, 111

Verdun, 22, 33, 38
  See also Metz, Toul, and Verdun
Vexaincourt, 134
Victim's privilege, 97-107
Vienna, 85
Voltaire, 50
Vosges mountains, 21, 24, 25, 82, 83, 84, 189
Vorwarts, 207

"Wackes," 190, 191
Wagner, Adolph, 93-94
Waltz, J J. *See* Hansi
War, 217, 222
Waterloo, 66
Wedel, Count von, 184, 206, 212
Werder, General von, 75, 118
Westphalia, treaty of, 36, 38, 39,

Wetterlé, Abbé, 162, 171, 172, 185
"Will to power," 85
William I, 89, 111, 124, 128, 136
William II, 7, 8, 136
  Quoted, 222
Windhorst, 119
Wissembourg, 32, 74, 173
Wittich, Werner, 184
Wörth, 74

Würtemberg, 32, 210
Würtemberg, Duke of, 58
Würtemberg, King of, 88–89, 91

"Young Alsace," 161, 162

Zabern. *See* Saverne
Zersplitterung, 31
Zislin, 159
Zweibrücken, Duke of, 58